WITCH

WITCH

The Wild Ride from Wicked to Wicca

Candace Savage

THE BRITISH MUSEUM PRESS

Text copyright © 2000 by Candace Savage
Illustrations copyright © 2000 as credited

First published in Canada by Greystone Books
A division of Douglas & McIntyre Ltd.

Published in Great Britain in 2001 by The British Museum Press
A division of The British Museum Company Ltd
46 Bloomsbury Street, London WC1B 3QQ

British Library Cataloguing in Publication Data
A catalogue record for this book is available from the British Library

ISBN 0-7141-2760-4

Every attempt has been made to trace accurate ownership of copyrighted visual material in this book. Errors
and omissions will be corrected in subsequent editions, provided notification is sent to the publisher.

Page viii: From *Roald Dahl's Revolting Rhymes* by Roald Dahl. Copyright © 1982 by Roald Dahl. Reprinted by
   permission of Alfred A. Knopf Children's Books, a division of Random House, Inc.
The silhouettes on pages xiv, 8, 18, 48, 58, 88, 98 and 104 are by Arthur Rackham, from his *Little Brother, Little
   Sister; Cinderella;* and *The Sleeping Beauty* (the latter courtesy of the de Grummond Children's Literature
   Collection, University of Southern Mississippi).
Front cover: The Spell by Francisco Goya, 1797–98. Museo Lazaro Galdiano, Madrid
Back cover: Library of Congress, LC-USZ62-95578
Cover design by Barbara Hodgson and Val Speidel
Interior book design by Val Speidel
Printed and bound in Hong Kong by C & C Offset Printing Co., Ltd.

Pages ii–iii: Witches' Sabbath,
or *Hexenversammlung,* was
painted in 1607 by Frans
Francken the Younger.
It offers a detailed view of
the activities of witches
and magicians, as they
were described in the
scholarly literature of
the period. *Kunsthistorisches
Museum, Vienna*

I guess you think you know this story.

You don't. The real one's much more gory.

The phoney one, the one you know,

Was cooked up years and years ago,

And made to sound all soft and sappy

Just to keep the children happy.

—Roald Dahl

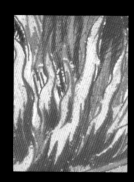

CONTENTS

HALLOWE'EN

PREFACE

I'll never forget the humiliating Halloween when I dressed up as a nurse. It snowed that night—cold and wet—and the red paper cross on my shoulder bled across my chest. I stood in the circle of light at someone's front door, singing for a treat, as my goody-two-shoes costume hung limply around my knees. They had to ask what I was supposed to be.

Never again, I vowed, and the next year I returned to my preferred cast of characters: gypsy or witch, witch or gypsy. Given what I now know about the heritage of both these images, this choice of personae, even in fun, makes me catch my breath. But at the age of ten, I had no idea that I was shouldering centuries of oppression, judicial murder and high-minded mockery. Instead, I was attracted by the icy power that radiated from both figures: the power of angry cursing and ill-tempered laughter, of forbidden knowledge, of fear. Bad-girl power.

No one asked what I was when I went as a witch. Nobody made me sing.

The Halloween witch's badge of authority was her hat, and my mother made the best in the world. There was a wonderful cunning in her hands when she fashioned one of them, miraculously fitting a tar-paper brim to a cone that rose to a point like a rapier. It was one of the many domestic miracles she performed for us each day—like making baking-powder biscuits without a recipe. When my sisters and I

Portrait of the author as a young witch.

Facing page: This Halloween postcard dates from around 1910. *David and Michele Hargis*

asked her how she achieved this culinary feat, she'd smile wryly and say, "It's magic." But how had she learned, we pressed her. "The witch in the mirror taught me."

Even after we'd decoded her joke (she used Magic-brand baking powder), my sisters and I loved this game of riddles. Sometimes, lined up in front of the living-room mirror to search for our mysterious benefactrice, we would find ourselves staring into the reflection of our mother's face. The witch in the mirror looked terribly sad.

Did we ask her why? Did we anxiously protest that she was not a witch, not really? Did she answer us? Somehow we came to understand that the mirror had caught a glimpse of our mother's private darkness. Even as she played and laughed with us, she could not let herself forget that she had sometimes failed to lived up to her own high standards of motherhood. The unpardonable fault lay in her witch anger, her witch violence, her witchy self-hatred.

In her own mind, she was the wicked stepmother of all the fairy tales she had ever, lovingly, read to us. Darkness answered darkness: I was sometimes sulkily sure that I had been adopted. I imagined I had two mothers, the one lovely as the sun by day, the other warty and cruel by night.

I tell you these stories because they are my own. They hint at the profound ways in which the myth of the witch continues to haunt women's lives and relationships. Your stories will be different from mine but I am willing to warrant that they are no less significant. For better or for worse, the witch is a fiction that we embody as fact, a phantasm that intrudes on our most intimate bonds, a negative space around which we give form to our selves. An anachronism with her roots in a bleak past, she is as contemporary as last night's bad dream. Pure make-believe, the witch nonetheless makes us believe that she is a force to be reckoned with.

Witches cause alarm and confusion wherever they appear, and the conception of this book has been no exception. Who and what was my subject? The gap-toothed little girls in pointy hats who showed up on my doorstep each Halloween, hoping for chocolate bars? The wicked stepmothers and evil fairies who had wrought havoc in the fairy tales of my childhood? The playful questing women and men with whom I'd sung and danced and made magic at witches' camps? Or was the real witch to be found in history, in the women (and children and men) who were tortured, hanged and burned at the beginning of the modern era?

"The witch runs away with Wild Rose." This illustration by H. J. Ford appeared in *The Crimson Fairy Book* in 1903. *Florence Collection*

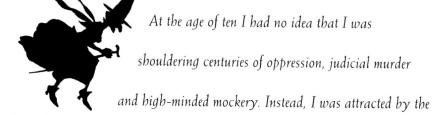

At the age of ten I had no idea that I was shouldering centuries of oppression, judicial murder and high-minded mockery. Instead, I was attracted by the power of angry cursing and ill-tempered laughter, of forbidden knowledge, of fear. Bad-girl power.

Was the witch fact or fiction? A superstitious "old wife" or a pagan priestess? A manifestation of sex hatred or a mythic figuration of women's resistance and power? Could she possibly be all of the above? And if so, how was this thinkable? How could the single word "witch" represent such an array of incompatible histories, meanings and emotions?

These are small questions in themselves, but they invoke larger mysteries of social change, gender identity and life in the image-saturated world of the twenty-first century. If it had not been for the trail of intellectual bread crumbs left by scholars like Christina Larner, Marina Warner, Norman Cohn, Robert Muchembled and the others who are listed in my bibliography, I would have been completely lost in these dark woods. I owe these people an enormous debt. It is also a pleasure to acknowledge the contributions of David and Michele Hargis, who gave me access to their collection of Halloween post-cards, and Gretchen A. Adams of the Department of History at the University of New Hampshire, who reviewed the manuscript. Finally, I am deeply grateful for the skill and friendship of my editor, Shelley Tanaka, and the intelligence and love of my two household "famil-iars"—my daughter, Diana Savage, and my companion (and consul-tant-in-residence), art historian Keith Bell.

Facing page: The wicked witch has troubled the imagination of the western world for the last five hundred years. *Peabody Essex Museum, Salem, MA*

SECRETS of a Shapeshifter

She dips her pen in terror. Will ye shrink?

Horace Walpole, The Mysterious Mother, 1768

Sometime in the late 1990s, a cherub-cheeked fourteen-year-old named Sarah slipped into her local Wiccashoppe and picked up a bottle of Love Potion Number 4. (The proprietor refused to sell her Love Potion Number 9, on the grounds that it was too powerful for teenagers.) Following the instructions for daily use that were printed on the vial, she dabbed the stuff on her wrists and heart and—more to the point, perhaps—focused her thoughts on the kind of guy she hoped to attract. Sure enough, a few weeks later he turned up in the flesh: blond, blue-eyed, skateboarding proof that her magical powers had been up to the task.

In the eyes of the journalist to whom she recounted this coup, Sarah appeared to be a typical member of "Generation Hex," one of those "perky pretty girls with butterfly pins in their hair" who were attracted to witchcraft as a way of adding "a little magical oomph to their budding Girl Power." Sarah the Teenaged Witch was far from sinister.

Five hundred years earlier, a young Venetian woman named Gratiosa had felt a similar need for erotic "oomph." In the absence of a corner shoppe, she engaged the assistance of two other women to brew a do-it-yourself concoction of rooster heart, wine, flour and menstrual blood, which (reduced to a powder) must have gone off the nine-point scale for potion power. Her admirer, to whom she fed the stuff, was inflamed with passion for her, despite the impossible difference that lay in their path. He was a nobleman; she, a commoner.

Facing page: The wonder— and the horror—of witch- craft is captured in this Scene of Sorcery, *which was conjured up by painter Léonard Defrance in the eighteenth century. Musée de l'Art Wallon de la Ville de Liège*

✦ 1

Regardless of this barrier, the lovers' hearts were light. Gratiosa playfully made a potion from their belly-button lint, which they drank in bed. She measured her lover's penis against a candle that was to be lighted at Mass in honor of their union. Even after all these years, we can almost hear her laugh.

But Gratiosa's happiness was suddenly quenched when the authorities learned of the affair and hauled the pair into court. Although her lover was judged to have committed many "sad stupidities," it was Gratiosa and her magic that bore the burden of blame. Convicted of sorcery, she was branded three times on the cheeks, fined and expelled from the city. If she ever dared to return, the court decreed, her nose was to be cut off.

In the Renaissance, the brewing of potions and poisons was thought to be a natural extension of women's work in the kitchen. The hand that stirred the soup by day might toil over a witches' cauldron after dark. *Dover Pictorial Archive*

The distance between the stories of Sarah and Gratiosa is the subject of this book. It is the distance between the present and the past. Between comedy and tragedy. Between innocent pleasure and cold brutality. These differences, in all their complexity and contradiction, cannot be easily bridged. Yet they come together in a single word, a single over-burdened female figure. The witch.

The witch is a figure that prickles with difficulty. One might almost be tempted to think of her as an archetype, one of those timeless and universal forms that, according to Carl Jung, provide the basic structure of the unconscious mind. Perhaps (as Jungian thought suggests) all humans are born with a vague, non-verbal "thought" of the bad mother, the evil woman, or of troublesome female power, which takes

on the shape and coloring of each successive culture and era in which it is expressed. If the concept of the witch is ambiguous, that may simply reflect the unbounded nature of an archetype. The Renaissance was terrified by witchcraft, and even today we may find the subject disconcerting. Underlying these varying responses is a deeply human unease with dark and subversive aspects of femininity. Or so Jung and many of his followers would have us believe.

True? False? Who can say? One thing we know for sure is that Jung's ideas cannot help us clarify our thinking. The female-witch archetype (if it exists) inhabits an ethereal world of ambiguities and abstractions, somewhere off in the clouds, where the slap of a skateboard or the hiss of a branding iron has never been heard. The notion of the witch that concerns us exists in history, in the ordinary, hour-by-hour progression of events through which the present turns into the past. Even more specifically, our witch belongs to the history of western culture over about the last five hundred years—from the end of fifteenth century (when Gratiosa was condemned) until the dawn of the twenty-first (when Sarah went shopping). How did we get from There to Here—from the terror of the Renaissance witch-craze to the inspired playfulness of Wicca?

At the heart of this question lies an atrocity—between fifty and one hundred thousand people who were murdered by church and state,

For centuries, the casting of love spells was assumed to be a female speciality. In this engraving by the nineteenth-century French artist Galvarni, two young women have retreated to the forest, where they are casting secret ingredients into their philtre, or love potion. *Jean-Loup Charmet*

In Scotland, a witch craze ignited in 1590, when King James VI became convinced that his political enemies had invoked the Devil against him. His suspicions flamed into panic when his ship was caught in a storm as he was bringing his bride home from Denmark. *Bibliothèque nationale de France*

for a crime that most of us would now judge to have been illusory. (Although figures as high as nine million deaths have been mentioned in the past, these are not supported by the evidence.) Eighty per cent of those who died were women and girls; the majority of them were old and friendless; almost all were poor. Countless others, like Gratiosa, barely escaped with their skins to eke out lives disfigured by shame. And this perversion of justice occurred not in some imagined Dark Ages of barbarous superstition, but in the sixteenth and seventeenth centuries, at the height of that great flowering of European culture we call the Renaissance. When the witches in *Macbeth* first muttered into their cauldron on the stage of the Globe theater in 1611, real-life "witches" were dangling from gallows or writhing on pyres across western Europe. Although the witchpanic began in the mid-1400s, it peaked between about 1580 and 1630, with late outbreaks in Sweden in the 1680s and in Salem, Massachusetts, ten years afterwards. The last person to be executed for witchcraft in western Europe—Anna Göldi by name—died in Switzerland in 1782.

Exactly who these "witches" were and why they died are questions to trouble the human heart. But in the immediate aftermath of their deaths, the answers had seemed easy. To the proponents of science who were on the rise as the witch craze began to wane, the whole sad affair

A woman beset by demons—and hence at risk of becoming a witch—is pictured in this tender and terrifying drawing by sixteenth-century artist Raffaellino da Reggio. *British Museum*

Counting Bodies

In a sense, it is correct to think of the western European witch craze as one big pogrom. From England to Italy and Poland to Spain, the crime of witchcraft was defined and prosecuted in much the same way. But what did differ dramatically from one jurisdiction to the next was the ferocity with which the law was enforced. In some countries—including England, Spain, Italy, Poland, Sweden and the Netherlands—outbreaks of panic were short-lived and the death rate was relatively low. In England, for example, fewer than five hundred people were killed; but across the border in Scotland, more than one thousand victims were drawn from a much smaller population. Scotland's tragedy stemmed from the use of torture in its courts (a practice that was not permitted in England), the intense religious fervor of its church and the political anxieties of an insecure monarch. (The young King James VI lived in constant fear that his enemies were working black magic against his rule.) Similar forces were also at work in France, the Swiss confederacy and the many small German-speaking principalities of the day, all of which suffered intense and lasting panics. The worst atrocities occurred in the German lands where between the fifteenth and eighteenth centuries some twenty-five thousand to fifty thousand people were burned—half of all the lives that were lost to witch-hunters.

The engraver Jean Luyken memorialized the frightful deaths of eighteen persons at Salzburg in 1528.
Bibliothèque nationale de France

Left: In England, witches were hanged to death instead of being burned. Here, the women's demonic pets cavort beneath the gallows. *Dover Pictorial Archive*

appeared to be exactly what one would expect from a society that was immersed in "old wives' tales" and superstitious beliefs. Once the bright sun of reason had dissipated those foolish fears, humanity turned down a well-marked path towards civility and progress. Even before the tragedy of the witch craze had fully drawn to a close, Enlightenment thinkers were telling themselves that no such travesty could ever again occur in their bright-and-shiny, thoroughly modern world.

A hundred years later, in the mid-1800s, this enviable confidence had still not begun to dim, but many thinkers were beginning to express doubts about the Enlightenment's infatuation with rationality and science. Rather than submit to the chilly order of Voltaire, Newton and Locke, the Romantics favored the oracular splendors of the imagination. As they cast their dreamy, moonlit gaze back over the past, they became transfixed by the aura of magical possibility that surrounded the witch craze. The women who had been killed could not have been superstitious fools, as Enlightenment scholars had thought; surely they must rather have been vessels of ancient inspiration, carriers of timeless knowledge, rebels against the strictures of Christian dogma (as were the Romantics themselves). The witches were now reimagined as visionaries, oracles and glorious *femmes fatales*, who had been victimized by dark forces of prudery and oppression.

With a wave of their magic wands, the Romantics gave the witch a

In this detail from *Witches and Their Incantations*, Salvator Rosa imbues a dark and fantastic scene with the sheen of flesh-and-blood reality. The painting, which dates from the 1640s, served to confirm the murderous beliefs of the witch hunters. *National Gallery of England*

Watch and before your very eyes, presto chango, a capital crime of the most hideous sort will be turned into a superstition, then into an inspiration, then again into an act of resistance. A public enemy will morph into a halfwit, the halfwit into a muse, the muse into a role model.

new spin. And once spun, the image of the witch just went on spinning. In time, the Romantics' witch would be taken up by the women's movement of the nineteenth and twentieth centuries and transformed into a holy martyr of feminism. Now the women who died as witches were to be reclaimed as sisters who had offended the patriarchal establishment; as healers and midwives who had been persecuted by the male medical establishment; as goddess worshippers who had felt the full ferocious opposition of the clergy. This was powerful mythmaking—a Number 9 on any scale—and it has inspired many of us in our quest for affirmation and guidance.

For the moment, the point is not to ask whether these varying depictions of the witch are true or false (though the facts will emerge in due course). What matters now is simply to observe this spectacle of cultural transformation. Watch and before your very eyes, presto chango, a capital crime of the most hideous sort will be turned into a superstition, then into an inspiration, then again into an act of resistance. A public enemy will morph into a halfwit, the halfwit into a muse, the muse into a role model. Back in the Renaissance, people believed that witches were shapeshifters, capable of surprising transformations from human to animal and from specter to flesh and blood. Extending this idea metaphorically, we can see that the idea of the witch has been constantly shifting shape, on its long and wild ride through western history.

It is the layering, one on top of the other, of these various "shapes" that makes our understanding of the witch so contradictory and complex. Each image recalls a position in an historical debate, which may originally have centered on the nature of evil or reality or human con-

sciousness. Yet each of these positions is represented by an image of a witch, which is to say, of a human female. Every time the witch has morphed into a new form, this shift has had real-life consequences for women and girls. In the beginning, as we all know, those consequences were terror.

The story of the witch that I am going to tell you begins with an outrageous abuse of power, of a kind that will be recognizable to anyone who has contemplated the atrocities of our own era. This telling is based on my reading of an impressive new body of historical studies of the witch craze that invites us to reconsider virtually everything we thought we knew about this bewildering episode. For a start, this scholarship suggests that the idea of the female witch was largely the work of spin doctors. Rather than emerging authentically from medieval folk culture, the witch was the brain child of theologians, lawyers and other intellectuals who (with the deepest sincerity) conjured her up to satisfy their own political and cultural needs. Exactly how the witch-mongers cast their spell, and what their purposes may have been, is the subject we will turn to in the next chapter.

Halloween witches soar over the sleeping streets of Salem, Massachusetts, in 1895. Yet only a few generations before, a nightmarish vision of witchcraft had troubled this same quiet town and provoked its citizens to violence. Through the alchemy of history, a horrifying danger had somehow been transformed into a playful illusion. (This illustration was used to advertise a cosmetic "witch-cream" that promised to work wonders.) *Peabody Essex Museum, Salem, MA*

CONJURING *a Nightmare*

*All wickedness is but little
to the wickedness of a woman.*

Ecclesiasticus XXV

What got his Lordship most worked up was the women's hair. The way it flowed across their shoulders and shimmered in the light, as "violent" as a sunburst in a stormy sky. The way it framed their eyes—such fascinating eyes—"as dangerous in love," he tells us, "as in witchcraft."

It is not far, as the crow flies, from Bordeaux to the Basque coast of southwestern France, but for Judge Pierre de Rosteguy, Sieur de Lancre, those few days' travel in the summer of 1609 had been a transport to a new and disquieting world. He had seen his share of marvels in his fifty-six years—the time in Rome, for instance, when the Devil had transformed a girl into a boy before his very eyes. Yet, as he admits in his book about his adventures, nothing had prepared him for this encounter with the Basque peasants. They were just poor fishing folk, bashed and buffeted by the sea, but far from being cowed by hardship, they conducted themselves with haughty self-assurance, calling each other "Lady This" and "Sir That" and refusing to bow to the routine of agricultural work.

As for those glowing Basque women, surely they were trouble in the flesh. Left to their own devices for six months of the year while their fathers and husbands fished the Grand Banks of Newfoundland, they enjoyed what looked to de Lancre like outrageous independence. What was it the old textbooks had said? "When a woman thinks alone, she thinks evil." And here were women, freed from the discipline of

Facing page: If a man found a woman attractive—if she tempted him to sin— that was a sign she was in league with Satan. According to an authoritative book on witchcraft, women were nothing but "a natural temptation, a desirable calamity, a domestic danger, a delectable detriment, an evil of nature, painted with fair colors." *Detail from* Witches' Sabbath *by Frans Francken the Younger, 1607, Kunsthistorisches Museum, Vienna*

✦ 11

men, who not only thought evil but dared give voice to it. Some of them had recently become so bold as to speak out against a local nobleman, and he had retaliated by having several of the older women arrested on charges of witchcraft. The penalty for those convicted would be death at the stake, and it was up to de Lancre—on an emergency commission from King Henry IV—to prosecute and incinerate the guilty parties.

From the moment of his arrival, de Lancre kept his population of suspects under keen surveillance. He saw how the young women and boys cruised back into the village each afternoon, no doubt whispering about their secret trysts up in the hills. How the women danced away half the night to the jangle of tambourines, as sensual and shameless as gypsies. How the priests, contrary to God's own decency, permitted mere females to approach the altar, view the elevation of the host and carry the chalice during Mass.

De Lancre immediately recognized what he had stumbled upon. Sent to deal with a few isolated cases of evil-doing, he found himself confronted with a vast Satanic conspiracy that appeared to involve most, perhaps even all, of the thirty thousand people in the Basque country.

When Pierre de Lancre looked at the Basque women, all he could think of was sex. But another contemporary observer, Gregorio Houfnaglio, remained more detached. Where de Lancre saw a population of sirens, Houfnaglio noted normal, high-spirited women with distinctive customs and dress. In particular, he drew attention to the unusual horned headdress worn by married women, right, and the unbound hair of the unmarried girls, left. *Musée Basque*

Not everyone would accept this conclusion, as de Lancre knew only too well. His own wife's late uncle, the wit and essayist Michel de Montaigne, had been among those to express their skepticism. "It is rating our conjectures too highly to roast people alive for them," Montaigne had cautioned.

But, surely, de Lancre's assessment of the Basque women was more than conjecture. Even in this century of bloodshed and dissent, when Catholic stood against Protestant and reformer against traditionalist—when matters of doctrinal difference were being fought out on battlefields across Europe—a few precious truths had emerged as self-evident. Who could now doubt, for instance, the proper place of women in God's grand scheme? The leading theologians of all the major factions spoke with one voice on this theme, extolling the feminine virtues of piety, self-sacrifice and chastity within marriage. As long as woman stayed close to her hearth, tending meekly to husband and kin, civilization was assured. But if she overstepped these limits, the balance would inevitably tip toward chaos.

It took no special genius to see that the unbridled women of the Basque were in league with the powers of darkness. All that remained for de Lancre was to prove in court that these creatures had literally allied themselves with the Devil.

The basic tenets of witchcraft law were well established and clear. A witch was any person—more often than

The importance of keeping women in their place was a popular theme for artists in the fifteenth and sixteenth centuries. This engraving shows the philosopher Aristotle reduced to humiliating submission by the seductive Phyllis. *From* Late Gothic Engravings of Germany & the Netherlands *by Max Lehrs, Dover, 1969*

BORDER CROSSINGS

Sadly, we know very little about the people who were convicted of witchcraft by Pierre de Lancre. The official records of the trials were destroyed in a fire in 1710, so the best surviving source is the judge's own report—a rambling, sensational, 600-page work on the perversity of the Devil. The only face of the "witches" that de Lancre wants us to see is bizarre and demonic.

For a more human side of the story, we need to slip across the border to the Basque region of northern Spain, where better records have been maintained. A similar panic broke out there in 1609, apparently sparked by refugees from the French side. Among them was a twenty-year-old serving maid named Maria de Ximildegui, who—with whatever motive—said that she had consorted with the

An Inquisitor, left, hears the testimony of a witch or unbeliever, far right, as *el secretario del Secreto* takes note of the proceedings. Despite its reputation for severity, the Spanish Inquisition actually practiced remarkable restraint in trying people accused of witchcraft. *Cornell University Library*

witches in France. (Was she an attention-seeker? Or had she become caught up in an epidemic of terrible dreams, as may have been the case with some of the women who gave evidence to de Lancre?) However it happened, Maria now offered to name Spanish women whom she claimed to have seen worshipping the Devil at witches' gatherings.

When these women were confronted with her accusations, several of them broke down. Maria de Jureteguia, for example, first fainted, then confessed. Pressed for more information, she offered up a list of other witches that included her own aunt. Arrested and thrown in prison, she was later heard to admit that her story had been fabricated from the outset. Once the word "witch" hung over a woman's head, a full and false confession might be her only chance.

For Maria de Jureteguia, this strategy proved wise—both she and her aunt escaped with their lives. The only suspects sentenced to death were six courageous souls who refused to admit their guilt. They were burned at the stake in November 1610, together with a Muslim, a Lutheran, six Jews and a dozen other enemies of the faith.

People condemned by the Spanish Inquisition were executed with pomp and circumstance at an *auto-da-fé*, or "act of faith." Public executions were intended to warn the population against straying from the truth.

Bibliothèque nationale de France

The *Compendium Maleficarum*, or *Compendium of Diabolical Magic*, was published in 1608 by a priest-turned-exorcist named Francisco Maria Guazzo. The text was amplified by numerous illustrations, which presented incredible happenings in matter-of-fact detail. Above, for example, we see a follower of the Devil accepting baptism from his infernal lord; below, another witch permits the Devil to mark him with a claw. *Dover Pictorial Archive*

not female—who had chosen to foreswear her Christian baptism and devote herself to the service of Satan. It was through this demonic connection that she obtained her powers to cause suffering and harm—to kill livestock, ruin harvests, spread disease and death, and generally inflict toil and trouble upon the populace. Yet obtaining proof of this compact was notoriously difficult, since the Devil was a wily and determined opponent. Time and again, he would silence the suspects' tongues to prevent them from speaking in court or force them to protest their innocence, in defiance of God's justice.

What choice did the judge then have except to call on his torturers and the painful persuasions of the thumbscrew, the rack and the strappado? And how could the court neglect its duty to lead witnesses to the truth, even if (as de Lancre acknowledged) aggressive "questioning . . . [was] merely a trick to trap" the accused.

As an agent of the king—and through the king, of God—de Lancre found himself in single combat with the Prince of Darkness, the only bulwark of civilization in an apocalyptic struggle against complete collapse. For did not the witches of the Basque threaten the entire chain of constituted authority, from husband to priest to monarch to the Deity Himself? For this very reason, wiser men than he had long recognized witchcraft as a *crimen exceptum*, an offense so heinous that the niceties of due process became irrelevant.

The Devil abducts a witch and takes her to a sabbat aboard a forked stick. In the background, a hailstorm brews as a result of the witch's evil magic. *Dover Pictorial Archive*

As for her alluring tresses, best to get rid of them—cut them off and shave the suspect's body, so she cannot hide the mark with which the Devil brands his converts.

Just get the job done and, for God's sake, watch yourself. Women, by their nature, are full of wiles and snares. Merely gazing into a witch's eyes can soften a judge's heart, inspiring such diabolical compassion that he is forced to let her go. As for her alluring tresses, best to get rid of them—cut them off and shave the suspect's body while you are at it, so she cannot hide the mark (usually an insensitive patch of skin that will not bleed when pricked) with which the Devil brands his converts.

Judge de Lancre plunged into his official tasks, hauling in women and girls by the dozens and then the hundreds to stand before his

A torturer is shown practicing his craft in this eloquent sixteenth-century woodcut. *Bibliothèque nationale de France*

How the truth was drawn from Françoise Secretain

"For three days of her imprisonment Françoise Secretain refused to confess anything, saying that she was innocent of the crime of which she was accused and that they did her great wrong to detain her. To look at her, you would have thought she was the best woman in the world; for she was always talking of God, of the Virgin Mary, and of the Holy Saints of Paradise, and she had in her hand a long rosary which she pretended to say without interruption. But the truth is that the Cross of this rosary was defective [as could be expected of a witch], and it will be seen that this fact furnished evidence against her.

"Further, it was observed that during her examination, although she strove her utmost to do so, she could not shed a single tear [again after the manner of witches]. For this reason she was more closely imprisoned, and certain threats were used to her. The following day she was pressed to tell the truth, but without success. Accordingly it was decided to shave off her hair and change her garments, and to search her to see if she were marked in any way. She was therefore stripped, but no mark was found; and when they came to cut the hair off her head she submitted with the utmost confidence. But no sooner was her hair cut than she grew perturbed and trembled all over her body, and at once confessed, adding to her first confessions from day to day."

From *An Examen of Witches* by Judge Henry Boguet, Burgundy, France, 1590

The wailing of dying women contends with the roar and crackle of the flames. This sketch by J.-J. Wick commemorates the deaths of nine "witches" who were convicted of causing an outbreak of plague in Geneva in 1571.

Zentralbibliothek Zurich

bench. The witnesses soon confirmed and surpassed his worst imaginings. Seventeen-year-old Marie Dindarte revealed that on the night of September 27, 1609, she had rubbed herself with flying ointment and rushed off to join other witches at a nighttime gathering, or sabbat. (Challenged to fly around the courtroom, she said could not do so because the Devil was displeased with her testimony and had refused to give her any more of the magical salve.) Marie de Marigrane, fifteen, and three of her friends had gone to a similar meeting in Biarritz, flying on the back of the Devil in the form of an ass. Other witnesses—many of them children and teenaged girls—reported that they were snatched nightly from their beds and transported on broomsticks, shovels or spits to attend mass gatherings in the public square of Bordeaux or way across the Atlantic in Newfoundland. Some claimed

The Devil, in the form of a goat, accepts the obscene tribute of his disciples at a witches' sabbat. In the background, flying witches intermingle with demons and owls, while on the margins of the scene, people shift into the shapes of cats and other beasts. *Bibliothèque nationale de France*

to have counted several hundred participants, including neighbors whom they incriminated by name to the court. Others multiplied the total to twelve thousand or even one hundred thousand. Anything to appease this terrible man who held their lives in his hands.

De Lancre was especially hungry for the dirty bits. He wanted to hear how the witches kissed the Devil's asshole and offered themselves to be whipped. He quizzed them about banqueting on dead babies and toads and dancing in the nude. He encouraged them to describe the sexual orgies in which women coupled with women, mothers with their sons. Under his questioning, the witches' sabbat was revealed as a carnival of depravity, a world turned upside down, in which participants literally stood on their heads to worship their perverted god. The climax of the ceremony was an act of sexual servitude, in which each participant offered herself to the Devil. De Lancre was eager to hear about the demon's huge, icy penis and scaly testicles.

Never before had the witches' sabbat been described in such lurid detail. Yet de Lancre could reflect with satisfaction that the evidence from his court was in close accord with the findings of other respected witch judges and theorists around Europe. Surely this proved beyond all shadow of doubt that, despite the Devil's lies, he had persevered to secure the facts. So when several of the convicted "witches" begged him to rehear their testimony—saying that they had spoken out of fear and their confessions were all lies—de Lancre knew better than to listen. Even when they implored him to tear up

German artist Hans Baldung Grien exploited the pornographic possibilities of witch imagery in his 1515 depiction of a woman accepting the sexual attention of a demon-dragon. *Staatliche Kunsthalle, Karlsruhe*

Pierre de Lancre's book about his strange adventures in the Basque country was so popular that it immediately went into a second printing. The new edition included an illustration by Polish-born printmaker Jan Ziarnko, which depicted key elements of the trial testimony. Witches are shown playing infernal music, dancing back to back, brewing storms, eating babies, inducting children into the cult and flying helterskelter on their brooms. *Cornell University Library*

their statements, lest their souls be damned for bearing false witness against the neighbors and friends whom they had named to the court, the judge stood fast for God's truth. As many as ten men and seventy women were sent to their deaths, and Pierre de Lancre returned to his home in Bordeaux with an easy conscience.

Anne Hendricks was fed to the flames in Amsterdam in 1571. *Bibliothèque nationale de France*

Facing page, top: In 1573, citizens of Haarlem were executed en masse for devoting themselves to Satan. *Dover Pictorial Archive*

Facing page, bottom: Engraver Erhard Schoen depicted the "Curious Execution of a Witch at Schilta" in 1533. *From The German Single-Leaf Woodcut:1500–1550 by Max Geisberg, Hacker Art Books, 1974*

If de Lancre's killing spree had been an isolated event, we would surely, after all these years, be ready to let it rest. Instead, what happened in southwestern France was repeated, with varying degrees of force, in virtually every principality and nation across western Europe at some time between about 1500 and 1700. For each person who was put to death in the Basque, another ten thousand would die elsewhere before the crisis shuddered to an end.

In a sense, the prosecution of witches was not startlingly new. Since the beginning of recorded history, the law had always taken a stand against black magic and its practitioners. As far back as 1300 BC, an Egyptian man named Penhaiben had been executed for stealing a magical book from his master and using it to cast harmful spells. A thousand years later, Roman law had exacted the same penalty for "soothsayers, enchanters, and those who make use of sorcery for evil purposes." Five hundred years after that, the laws of the Visigothic kingdoms had prescribed public whipping as the punishment for *tempestarii*, storm-making magicians who extorted money from farmers by threatening to hail their crops. And around AD 800, the great legal codifier Charlemagne had again assigned the death penalty for all

HAERLEM

those who "in any way invoked the devil, compounded love-philters, afflicted either man or woman with barrenness, troubled the atmosphere, excited tempests, destroyed the fruits of the earth, dried up the milk of cows, or tormented their fellow-creatures with sores and diseases"—exactly the charges that would later be laid against witches.

From kings to commoners, people had always dreaded the powers of evil sorcerers. Yet for three thousand years or more, that fear had never escalated into terror. Evil was afoot in the world; of that there could be no doubt. But throughout the early Middle Ages, the forces of darkness had seemed to be under control. Even without the help of the law, there were things a person could do to protect his or her life and livelihood. A bottle buried under the threshold of the house would keep away harmful spirits; a local "cunning man" or "wise woman"

In the sixteenth century, a woman who was troubled by demons also had reason to fear the torments of the justice system. In earlier periods, by contrast, the church had often attempted to assist people who fell prey to evil spirits. *Zentralbibliothek Zurich*

could be engaged to work a counter-spell against the influence of evil magic. Even the church could often be called upon for blessings and charms and, in the worst of emergencies, to exorcise anyone who had become possessed by Satan or one of a fabulous assortment of lesser demons.

As the Devil carries her off to Hell, a woman reaches toward her village church and its promise of help. *Dover Pictorial Archive*

If the medieval church was relatively unconcerned about evil magic in general, it was also remarkably unperturbed about the supernatural abilities attributed to women in particular. For centuries, the priests had been hearing reports of women who said that they had magical powers of flight, which they experienced in the dark of night. Yet for the longest time, the official response had been bemused disbelief; this had not been something that reasonable men were prepared to take seriously. In AD 906, for example, a bishop named Regino of Prüm had produced a manual to guide priests in the confessional, cataloguing all the sins to which the faithful might admit and providing each with an appropriate penance. Among these deviations, he reported on "certain wicked women" who said they rode out at night "with Diana the pagan goddess and a huge throng of women on chosen beasts. . . . They say that in the silence of the night they can traverse great stretches of territory, that they obey Diana as though she were their mistress and that on certain nights she calls them to her special service."

Other women reported adventures that were even more bizarre: they flew out of their beds—right through the walls—to kill and devour their neighbors. Yet no gnawed corpses were ever found, since the victims' lives were restored and morning found the self-professed

cannibals still in their husbands' arms. Other women said that they rose from their beds to fly up and fight, giving and receiving wounds that could be plainly seen in the next day's light.

To the priests in the Middle Ages who heard these confessions, the women's beliefs sounded like nothing more than foolish delusions. For as one of them put it, "Who is there who has not been taken out of himself in dreams and nightmares and seen in his sleep things he would never see when awake? Who is imbecile enough to imagine that such things, seen only in the mind, have a bodily reality?" The women were just having flying dreams, and although Satan was no doubt involved (as he was in all false beliefs), the priests did not think it necessary to

THE WILD HUNT

We will never hear directly from the women who rode out with the goddess in the tenth century. They flew through a world of stories that was sustained by word of mouth. Ironically, almost the only traces of their world that remain are fragments recorded by priests, in their tireless efforts to "correct" the old beliefs.

The priests were not deeply interested in what the women experienced or thought and took no special pains to ensure that they got things right. It may be, for example, that they introduced the name of Diana, Roman goddess of the hunt, because she was more familiar to them than the confusing local deities their parishioners mentioned—Holle, "the friendly one"; Berhta, "the bright one"; Epiphania, Satia and Abundia. All these figures were associated with the tradition of the "wild rout" or "wild hunt," which had originally been pictured as a nighttime procession of the dead.

The possibility that real live people—especially women—could join these spectral flights seems to have arisen early in the Middle Ages, but no one knows exactly where or why. Was this marvelous thought inspired by some new social trend—a revival of interest in shamanism and ecstatic soul-travel? An upsurge in the use of belladonna and other high-flying hallucinogens? Or was the idea of taking flight from life nothing more than romance, an irresistible dream of liberation and escape in the company of other women? And once this belief had arisen, why did it disappear, sometime around the year AD 1200? We will never know for sure.

Background: The Queen of the Wild Men was just one of the many figures that inhabited the minds of the common folk during the Middle Ages. To the priests, she was a delusion sent by Satan to lure people away from the truth. *From* Late Gothic Engravings of Germany & the Netherlands *by Max Lehrs, Dover, 1969*

THE FAIRY FAITH

When Chaucer's Wife of Bath entertained her fellow travelers on the road to Canterbury, sometime in the 1390s, she spoke of a wondrous time when fairies had danced in meadows and greens around England. But the fairies had already been gone for hundreds of years, she said, chased away by holy friars, "as thikkes as motes in the sonne-beam," who had hurried around the country blessing everything in sight. "This maketh that ther ben no fayeryes," she sighed.

But in a few more fortunate parts of Europe, the clergymen had been less thorough, and the fairy faith had outlived even the redoubtable Wife herself. In 1588, for example, a fisherman's wife in Palermo, Sicily, told how she and a company of women had flown on billy-goats to the fairy mountain of Benevento. There on a dias sat a beautiful lady and "a red young man," the queen and king of the fairies. The company kneeled before these deities and did everything they said, in the hope of receiving "wealth, beauty and young men to make love with." This worship was followed by a celebration of food, drink and joyful sex.

"All this seemed to her to be taking place in a dream, for when she awoke she always found herself in bed, naked as when she had gone to rest." When she told her confessor about her flights, he said her dreams had been the work of the Devil. But in spite of this she had continued her dream-journeys for a while, because they gave her such enjoyment.

Unhappily, these innocent pleasures were eventually criminalized. Between 1547 and 1701, this woman and sixty-four other daydream believers were tried by church courts in Sicily. These are the only known trials in which followers of the "fairy faith" were prosecuted for witchcraft.

Peasant women sometimes escaped into a joyful world of dreams, in which they feasted and danced with the fairies. But their confessors thought they had been consorting with demons instead, like these revellers at a witches' sabbat. *Bibliothèque nationale de France*

intervene forcefully. In the eleventh century, the recommended penance for a woman who confessed to flying around and eating human flesh was an annual fast of forty days for seven years in a row—altogether a far cry from being burned at the stake.

There were, however, two instances in which this wise toleration had abruptly lapsed. In the twelfth and thirteenth centuries, the church had taken up arms against two sects of dissident Christians in France—the Albigensians and Waldensians, by name—both of which had attracted a large female following. Unlike the established church, the dissenting movements allowed women to perform baptisms, give absolution and preside over the Mass—policies that must have gone a long way towards explaining their success. But these innovations (among others) put the church into a blind rage, and the adherents of both sects were condemned as heretics. To discredit the reformers in the eyes of the public, the prosecution had them tortured until they confessed to appalling crimes, such as copulating with demons, flying through the night, eating human infants and spreading the Black Death. With this "proof" in hand, the church courts then sentenced them to burn en masse.

When its power was at risk, it seemed, the church was prepared to believe whatever was necessary. Heretics, it had now been proved, could actually consort with devils in the flesh and fly across vast distances on goats and broomsticks. These weren't just dreams; they were plain facts, as sanctioned by the Holy Catholic Church. So, sometime later, when rumors began to circulate that a new cult of night-flying heretics had appeared in the Swiss Alps (in the very

Background: Part woman, part beast, three demonic creatures prepare to take flight. *Dover Pictorial Archive*

valleys where the Waldensians had eventually found refuge), these stories were received with more credence than we might expect.

This terrifying new cult of sorcerers was first fully exposed in 1486 by two prominent German clergymen, the Dominican Heinrich Kramer, one-time spiritual director of the cathedral at Salzburg, and his co-author, Father James Sprenger, dean of theology at the University of Cologne. Their book, *Malleus Maleficarum*, or *Hammer of the Witches*, provided the first comprehensive guide to identifying, inter-rogating, torturing—and burning—members of the new sect, and as such, it enjoyed an enormous distribution and renown. Over the decades, it would appear in multiple editions in several languages and for many years would outsell every other book except the Bible.

As visionaries and prophets with a warning for Mankind, Kramer and Sprenger were unwilling to be limited by mere facts. Not for them a dull recitation of the actual trials in the Alps, where concern had lately focussed on a male magician named Staedelin. Instead, Kramer and Sprenger were concerned with the deeper truths that underlay mundane events, and the real problem as they saw it was women. The *Malleus Maleficarum* was the first book to make the case that society was menaced by a cult of Devil-worshippers who, for the most part, were female.

This was a painful issue, but Kramer and Sprenger approached it with manly directness, for the proper "admonition," as they put it, of the "fragile feminine sex": "It has often been proved by experience that [women] are eager to hear of [this matter], so long as it is set forth with discretion." In their view, women became witches because they

The first known illustra-
tions of women flying
on poles and brooms
appeared in the 1450s.
Bibliothèque nationale de France

Facing page: This illumination from *The Crime of the
Waldensians* shows mem-
bers of the sect paying
homage to the Devil in
the form of the goat.
Overhead, their coreli-
gionists hover in the air
on the backs of demonic
dirigibles. *Bibliothèque royale
Albert 1ᵉʳ, Brussels ms. 11209,
folio 3 recto*

were, by their very nature, defective. Formed from a crooked rib ("bent as it were in a contrary direction to man"), females were "imperfect animals" compared to males, with a complete run of intellectual, spiritual and emotional weaknesses. Hence women were stupid, impulsive and easily swayed; they were unstable, deceitful and prone to vengeful rage. Yet despite their innate disabilities, the daughters of Eve refused to be governed by their natural sovereign—man. A woman would follow her own errant will "even to her own destruction," Kramer and Sprenger warned. Ambition was the besetting sin of wicked women.

But woman's final, fatal flaw—the shortcoming that opened her irredeemably to the seductions of evil—lay in her sexual charms. For what is woman but a tool of the Devil, luring man to the cesspits of sin? "All witchcraft comes from carnal lust," our celibate authors thunder, "which is in women insatiable." Because the "mouth of the womb" is always ravening for satisfaction, women will even lie with demons "for the sake of fulfilling their lusts." Small wonder then that they are willing to submit to Satan himself and enter his service as witches. Small wonder that like the heretics of old, they soar through the night mounted on many-horned goats (a traditional symbol of lust) or on broomsticks greased with the Devil's own ointment.

Kramer and Sprenger had mixed up an unholy brew, combining a

According to the authors of the *Malleus Maleficarum*, vanity was yet another female weakness. *Dover Pictorial Archive*

generous measure of monkish woman-hatred with a dollop of folk belief, a pinch of heresy and more than a soupçon of prurient fantasy. The result was an image of the sorceress that was startling in its originality. Suddenly, the darkness swarmed with malevolent women riding on spindles and brooms. And in their midst, one could discern a grotesque gathering of their shadowy half-sisters. Among them were the *strix* or lamiae, women who (in classical literature) had taken the form of owls and fed on the flesh of innocent children. Now that the nature of witchcraft had been defined, the kinship was brutally clear. *Strix* were witches; witches were *strix*. And similar conclusions could be drawn about virtually every other deviant female in all of history: the Jewish Lilith, first wife of Adam, who had flown off and become a demon rather than submit to male rule. The monstrous Circe, who had transformed Ulysses' crew into animals. Even the fabulous followers of Diana, who had once swept through the night skies. These figures and many others—whatever their source, whatever their differences—were instantaneously gobbled up by the rapacious new definition. Fresh-hatched though she was, Kramer and Sprenger fattened their witch on a diet of timelessness.

Yet, despite the vigor of the new theory, not everyone was convinced. In fact, when Kramer turned up in Innsbruck to pursue his witch-hunting in the 1480s, the local bishop had him run out of town

Francisco Goya's *The Spell*, which he painted around 1797, shows a conjurer (in the yellow robe) trying to draw a frightened woman under her control. A critic of the witch craze, Goya nonetheless drew on the traditional imagery of owl-light, bat-wing and mangled babies in his evocation of terror. *Museo Lázaro Galdiano, Madrid*

as a "senile old man." Even Sprenger deserted the cause to devote his energy to promoting the adoration of the Virgin—a project that helped keep ordinary women in their place without the trouble of bringing them to trial. By the early sixteenth century, Kramer and Sprenger's work had fallen into a brief eclipse, as if it were just another obscure and irrelevant oddity of medieval scholarship.

In their prime, Kramer and Sprenger had preached against the gathering gloom at the end of time. It was in this "twilight and evening of the world," they wrote, with sin "flourishing on every side and in every place," that the witches had begun to multiply. And, in a sense, they were right to fear the ultimate catastrophe, for the world as they knew it was about to be destroyed. The first tremors of the impending apocalypse were felt in 1517, when a monk named Martin Luther nailed a list of demands to the door of the cathedral in Wittenberg. As everyone who has survived a high-school history class will likely recall, this simple action sparked a reform movement that shook the Christian church and led to the schism between Catholics and Protestants. But that was not the half of it.

The Reformation began as a movement to cleanse the church of "pagan" superstition. Christianity had been corrupted by Satan, the Protestants said, and they found his mark even on the Mass, which they mocked as so much "hocus-pocus." (This was a sneering reference to the phrase with which the priest announced the transformation of the communion wafer into the body of Christ.) But correcting matters of doctrine was

The perfection of the Virgin stood in painful contrast to the sins and imperfections of all other women. *From* Late Gothic Engravings of Germany & the Netherlands *by Max Lehrs, Dover, 1969*

only the first step in the crusade. Taking the battle to the streets added a whole new degree of difficulty. Reform-minded clergy of all stripes, both Catholic and Protestant, agreed that the common people were wallowing in falsehood and sin, and that a distinct whiff of brimstone hung over all of them.

By the time of the Reformation, western Europe had been under Christian control for more than a thousand years, and the cults of the old pagan gods had long since disappeared. Yet the old ways still hung in the air, coalescing in strange stories and fantastic beliefs, and impregnating everyday life with unrepentantly pagan lust for pleasure. This sensibility was most joyfully expressed in the bawdy festivals with which the people marked the turning of the year—New Year, May's Eve, Midsummer, the Feast of Fools and the twelve long and lusty days of Yule. Chief among the celebrations was Carnival, which stretched from just after Christmas straight through to Lent. Far from devoting themselves to a penitential scrutiny of their sins (as the godly thought they should), Carnival-goers debauched themselves with two or three months of eating, drinking, dancing, scandal and casual sex. The centerpiece of the festival was masquerade—women dressed as men, peasants as nobles, sinners as priests, humans as animals—in a parodic free-for-all that mocked the divinely appointed order of things. It was as if the common people had all been bewitched.

Where to begin? One obvious target for the reformers were the village magicians—that motley crew of diviners, wizards, unwitchers,

Everywhere they looked, the reformers saw the mark of the Devil. In their eyes, a group of women enjoying a simple meal bore a startling resemblance to a cabal of witches at an unholy feast. This representation of a witches' sabbat was published in 1485. *Cornell University Library*

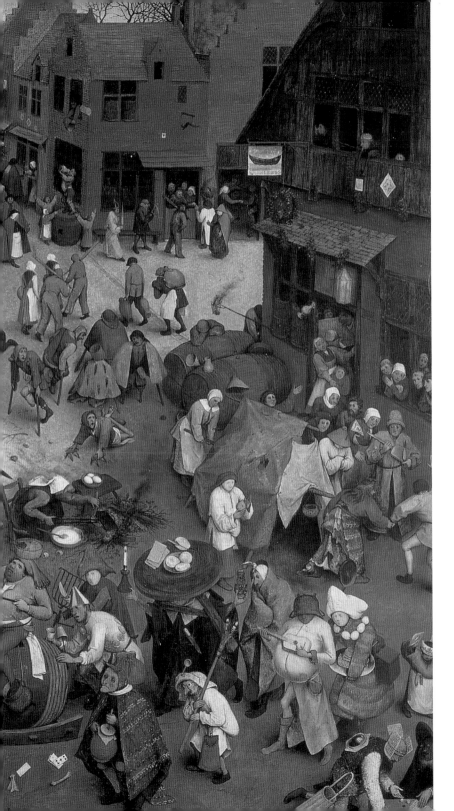

Pieter Bruegel's painting *The Fight Between Carnival and Lent* was created in the middle of the Reformation. It foregrounds the creative disorder of the people's celebrations, complete with drinking, dancing, masquerade and play-acting. But the grim-robed forces of repression are crowding into the scene through the open gateway and the back streets.

The Reformation represented the victory of Lent over Carnival. The witch-hunt was a particularly vicious aspect of the campaign to purify popular culture. *Kunsthistorisches Museum, Vienna*

faith healers, herbalists, cunning men and wise women, with their strange mumbo-jumbo of charms—to whom the country folk turned for healing, help in finding lost objects, and other assistance. This could no longer be tolerated. If people needed supernatural aid, they should be relying on authorized professionals within the church, not on this rabble of spiritual free-lancers. Even if they did not practice harmful magic, village healers were leading the people away from God and into the clutches of Satan. At their very best, they were nothing but "white witches," the reformers said, "the most horrible and detestable" of monsters.

The warnings of *Malleus Maleficarum* rang in the preachers' ears. "I should have no compassion on these witches," Luther declared. "I would burn all of them."

Meanwhile, out in the countryside, the people were burning with lust—another problem that required urgent attention. So missionaries were despatched across the continent to preach a somber new gospel of discipline and restraint. Women belonged within marriage, men belonged on top, and sexual pleasure was to be avoided at all costs. Anyone who deviated from this narrow path was at risk of landing in court. For at the same time as the witch craze reached its peak, the dockets were overflowing with charges of sodomy, bigamy, incest, abortion and other sexual crimes. As part of a vicious clamp-down on premarital sex, tens of thousands of women were charged with killing their illegitimate children. The penalty was death, and court records for the 1500s and 1600s suggest that nearly as many women in western Europe were killed for infanticide as for witchcraft.

Facing page: The preparation of medicines was a speciality of women. This medieval illumination shows two lay sisters preparing a remedy. *British Library, Royal 15 D IF 18*

AKING MAGIC

No matter how the preachers might rant about "white witches," the common people continued to trust the cunning folk and rely on their intercession. As a result, few village healers were ever prosecuted, because their clients were unwilling to testify against them. Many "white witches" continued to practice until the eighteenth century, when they were finally put out of business by medical licensing. Here is a small sampling of the charms that were used by village healers:

To prevent toothache, recite these words: "Peter was sitting on a marble-stone, and Jesus passed by; Peter said, 'My Lord, my God, how my tooth doth ache!' Jesus said, 'Peter art whole!' and whoever keeps these words for my sake shall never have the tooth-ache!'"

When gathering the herb vervain, say the following verse to ensure its potency: "Hail thou holy herb; growing upon the ground. / In the mount of Calvarie their was thou found. / Thou heallis manie greif, and stanches manie wound, / in the name of Sweit Jesus I tak thee from the ground."

To procure love: "Rubbe vervin in the bale of thy hande & rubbe thy mouth with it & immediatelye kysse her & it is done."

To avoid sex with demons: There is an old tradition "of a maide that liked well of the devill making love to her in the habit of a gallant young man, but could not enjoy his company, nor he hers, so long as shee had Vervine and S. Johns grasse [St. John's wort] about her."

Background: During the Reformation, the use of herbs (such as pennyroyal) to cause abortions was seldom mentioned in print. But the knowledge—which had been widely known during the Middle Ages—must still have been common among folk healers. Yet another reason for the clergy to distrust them.

Bildarchiv, ÖNB, Vienna

"Onward Christian soldiers, marching as to war." If the battle against Satan were to be won, women had to be brought into line. And any clear-sighted observer could see at once what God had in mind. "Men have broad shoulders and narrow hips," Luther once observed, a sure sign that they had been made for jostling their way through the world. But women, with their broad backsides, had been designed for sitting at home and looking after their husbands and children. The dour old Calvinist John Knox was even more direct: "Woman in her greatest perfection," he affirmed, "was made to serve and obey man." The only good woman in this brave new world was a chaste, stay-at-home wife, and anyone who resisted this dictum was kindling for God's purifying fire.

The female specters of *Malleus Maleficarum* had shuddered back to life, more troubling—more menacing—than ever before. They danced on the tongues of the preachers; they troubled the godly by night. They were out there by the thousands, sowing discontent and despair, from the fishing villages of the Basque to the farming towns of Bavaria. And each one of them was a warning to the people to reform their way of life: to reject superstitions, restrain their lust and keep one another under close surveillance. The witches came to trial as Public Enemy Number 1—the Devil in the shape of a woman.

Members of the medical profession, all male, are shown treating the victims of female witchcraft. This illustration appeared as a frontispiece in *Tractatus Physico-Medicus de Incantamentis* by G. A. Mercklin, 1715. *Cornell University Library*

OLD WIVES' Tales

I cannot see how any rationall man can persuade himself that a simple woman should doe such things as these.

Squire Henry Oxiden of Kent, England, 1641

The wicked witch had been conjured up as an act of war. She was a virtual weapon that passed across enemy lines, an intellectual Trojan horse that slipped, almost without notice, into the thoughts and dreams of the very people she was designed to chastise. Cunningly packaged to pass as a Genuine Folk Belief, the figure of the witch soon found her way into the tales and talk that were heard around the country markets and village hearths. Like a virus that infects a cell and turns it against itself, she invaded the common folk's hearts and persuaded them to focus their fears on one another.

Fear seeks for the vulnerable. The lonely. The aged. The poor. Fear of witchcraft focused on older women and widows. As one observer lamented, "Every old woman with a wrinkled face, a furr-d brow, a hairy lip, a gobber tooth, a squint eye, a squeaking voyce, or a scholding tongue . . . is not only suspected, but pronounced for a witch." In a century when scarcely one person in ten survived to their sixtieth year, age advanced apace, and most of the women charged as witches were by today's standards little more than middle aged.

Margaret Johnson of Lancashire, northern England, fit the type only too well—so well, in fact, that she

Facing page: To David Teniers the Younger, witchcraft seemed most at home within a frame of rustic country customs. *Hamburger Kunsthalle*

Suspicion of witchcraft often settled upon the poor. *Max Lehrs, Dover, 1969*

couldn't help but harbor suspicions against *herself*. It wasn't just her fifty-odd years that caused her anxiety, but her deep and abiding sadness. And she knew as well as anyone that this was exactly the emotional state that had driven so many women to take the Devil's hand. The cause might be the death of a child. A beating by a violent spouse. Even a trivial disagreement. In her own case (as in many others), the provocation had been a long series of nasty disputes and "vexations" with her "bad neighbours," as she called them. The worst of the lot had been a man named Henry Heap, who had driven her to distraction by slandering her as a witch. His accusations had caused

A woman who neglected her wifely duties aroused not only the ire of her husband but also the suspicions of her neighbors. *From* The German Single-Leaf Woodcut:1500–1550 *by Max Geisberg, Hacker Art Books, 1974*

Reality check

Thousands of documents survive from the witch trials of the sixteenth and seventeenth centuries. Yet in all this out-pouring of words, there is not one line that comes to us directly from the hand of any of the women who were condemned.

Apart from their tragic entanglement with the law, most of them seem to have lived quiet, unremarkable lives that have not left much trace in the archives. Judging from what little evidence we have, it appears that many of the accused were widows, most were over forty years of age, and virtually all were lower class or peasants. (Although wealthy women were occasionally charged, the cases against them rarely made it to court.) As for the men and boys who were drawn into the prosecutions, they were often the husbands, sons or defenders of female suspects.

Sometimes the enthusiasm for a witch-purge came from above, under the auspices of a zealot like Pierre de Lancre. But often the accusations flowed directly from the people themselves, as neighbors turned against one another. This was a world in which a person's life might literally depend on what the neighbors thought and said. Many of the women who were named as witches had been the subject of gossip for years and also stood accused of other offenses against "community standards": petty theft, sleeping around, arguing with men or living apart from their husbands. As a group, they seem to have been scrappy and strong-minded women, with scalding tongues that they loosed on anyone who dared to cross them. Whether or not they cast curses and spells (as some of them no doubt did), their neighbors were often relieved to get them out of their midst.

If a woman was "unnaturally" assertive, she often became the subject of vicious gossip. *From The German Single-Leaf Woodcut: 1500–1550 by Max Geisberg, Hacker Art Books, 1974*

her such despair that, soon afterwards, she had begun to yearn for Satan and his promise of revenge.

The Devil, she said, was a stylish young man called Mamilion, whom she had met on a lonely road and who had badgered her until she agreed to serve him, body and soul. Thereafter, he had visited her twice a week for sex (which she did not enjoy) and also to suckle blood from special teats that appeared on her genitals. In return for these services, she had received the power to curse and to kill, and Henry Heap, her enemy, had died because of her ill will. Or had she only thought to curse him after he was dead? Somehow, she couldn't be sure how it had happened.

In any case, a few months after Heap's demise, a witch craze flared

Here, two women engage in intense conversation about the ominous signs around them. In the background, hail beats on the rooftops, while a row of churns stands idle and useless. In the foreground, an old "witch" draws milk from an axe handle. *Cornell University Library*

up in Lancashire—more than a dozen people were charged—and, at the height of the excitement, Granny Johnson stepped forward to confess that she was a witch and a murderer. When her body was searched for witches' teats, an incriminating fold of skin was found "betwixt her seat and secrets"—positive proof that the Devil had sucked blood from her. In March of 1634, a jury decreed that Margaret Johnson was a Devil-worshipping witch and the killer, by bewitchment, of Henry Heap.

If the witch had started out as the brain child of the religious right, it was the simple folk in the country who brought the idea terribly to life. All the talk of diabolical witchcraft, in the pulpit and the pews, stimulated a fabulous flowering of folk belief, which might have been merely remarkable if it had not been so deadly. For Granny Johnson was not the only one who had taken the witch to heart; that year, the whole of Lancashire was buzzing with ghastly talk. Did you hear that Frances Dickenson had appeared to Edmond Stevenson the other week and troubled him when he was sick? If she wandered about as a specter, then surely she must be a witch. And Sharpee Smith had been saying that when Janet Loynd touched his cow, the animal had been cursed and afterwards was not even able to stand. As for Janet and William Device, whose mother and grandmother had both been hung as witches just twenty years before, there was little hope that they could avoid the curse of their ancestors.

A woman makes love with a bird-footed Devil.

Dover Pictorial Archive

FAMES 1575 SF

Whenever misfortune struck—a sheep died, a crop was ruined by hail, butter failed to churn—the villagers took it as yet more proof that the witches were at work. Fingers pointed; tongues whirred. Someone had to be to blame, and it was her . . . or him . . . or her.

Edmond Robinson was only ten when he made his own contribution to Lancashire lore, but despite his youth, he already knew what witches were for. When you were in trouble, they gave you someone to blame. So one day in the fall of 1633, he came rushing home—late—and regaled his parents with a spell-binding tale. It seemed that on his way out to the pasture, where he had been sent to get the cows,

In this depiction of famine, French artist Étienne Delaune has drawn on the equation between witchcraft and human suffering. *Bibliothèque nationale de France*

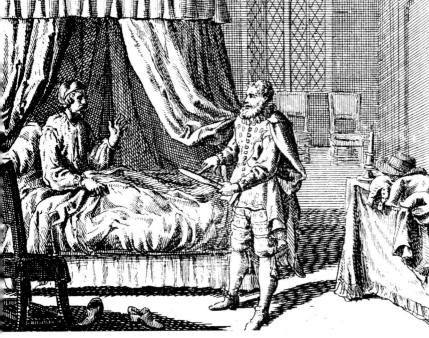

These panels, from a history of magic by R. Boulton, first appeared in 1715 with a caption that read: "The Duke of Buckingham's Death foretold by an Apparition." Above, we see the witch working her fatal magic with the aid of her demon helpers. Below, the poor doomed Duke is accosted in bed by a specter that the witch has sent to trouble him. *Peabody Essex Museum, Salem, MA*

he had unexpectedly encountered two greyhounds. Thinking to fit in a little hunting as he went along, he had set the dogs after a hare, only to discover that they would not chase it. (This was the first clue that something strange was afoot, since everyone knew that witches often turned themselves into rabbits.) Then, when Edmond started to beat the disobedient hounds, they were both instantly rans-

Old Women walk, fmoke and talk.

formed, one into Frances Dickenson, the suspected witch, and the other into a strange child.

Finding herself unmasked, the witch had tried to buy Edmond's silence by offering him a coin, but he had bravely refused (being a good boy). At this, she had produced a magic bridle that turned her strange companion into a white horse and, with Edmond perched in front of her, she had galloped off to attend a witches' banquet. Every-one you'd have expected to see had been present, Edmond said, not just Frances Dickenson but also Janet Loynd, Janet and William Device, the beggar Widow Beawse and all the others who had featured as witches in the village gossip. When Edmond had tried to run away home, he had run afoul of a boy who had bloodied his face and ears, "and looking down he saw the Boy had a cloven foot." The very Devil.

To people who were versed in the local witch lore, Edmond's story cried out for belief. He had entered a weird, otherworldly realm, and strange though it might seem, everything he had seen was in line with the talk that hissed (louder now than ever before) up and down the

These likenesses of village personalities were sold on the streets of London in the eighteenth century.

Dover Pictorial Archive

winding lanes of Lancashire. Even the fantastical bit where he went into a barn and saw witches pulling on ropes, from which meat and butter and milk came flying down, was not open to dispute. The very same facts had come out in the Device case, all those years before, and had stood as evidence in a court of law. Edmond's parents came to believe him and so did their neighbors and friends; soon his fame had spread to the neighboring parishes. With his father's sponsorship, he toured the country churches telling his sensational tale and then (for a fee) standing up to inspect the congregation, to see if he could identify any more of the people who had been at the witches' feast. Eventually, he made a sworn statement before two justices of the peace—naming names—and the machinery of criminal justice ground into gear.

It was in the midst of this hubbub that Granny Johnson felt moved to confess, and she and sixteen others (including Dickenson, Loynd, Beawse and Janet and William Device) were ultimately sentenced to die.

In the general run of witch cases, the story would have ended there, with a row of pathetic corpses hanging from the gallows. The jury had spoken, and the community (which had known that these people were guilty even before the trial began) accepted the outcome with gruesome satisfaction. But the circuit-court judges who had come in for the trial were not completely convinced. Except for Granny Johnson, none of the

The ability of witches to lull their victims to sleep —or throw them into a trance—was documented by the author of the *Compendium Maleficarum*. In this vignette, three well-dressed witches brandish sleeping potions above the bed of their dream-laden victim.

alleged witches had admitted their guilt. Instead of calling for the hangman, the judges arranged for the case to be reviewed by the highest court in the land: the Privy Council in far-away London. In June of 1634, four of the convicted women, along with Edmond and his father, were shipped south to be re-examined.

London was not Lancashire. The capital had sophistication, a kind of big-city cool; yet even here, the Lancashire witches were sensational news. People paid to stand and gawk when the women were put on display outside their cells at the Fleet prison. Street vendors did a brisk business hawking penny-pamphlets that promised titillating details about "The Witches Dance" or their alluringly unspecified "Prophane Pastime." At nearby Oxford, the "tricks" and "meetings" of the witches were played out with marionettes, and at London's Globe theater, a five-act romp entitled "The Late Lancashire Witches" became the blockbuster hit of the summer.

Written by two of city's most successful dramatists, Thomas Heywood and Richard Brome, "The Late Lancashire Witches" was quite the yuck-fest. Witches were good for the box office, as innocent women were not, so—despite the doubts that had brought the women to town—the play took full advantage of the testimony against them. Step right up and for the price of a cheap seat, you can watch Granny Johnson

The witches in Shakespeare's *Macbeth* first cast their spell over London theater in the early 1600s. The public's fascination with witchcraft was also fed by plays like Marlowe's *Dr. Faustus* and Jonson's *The Masque of Queenes. Delacroix, Bibliothèque nationale de France*

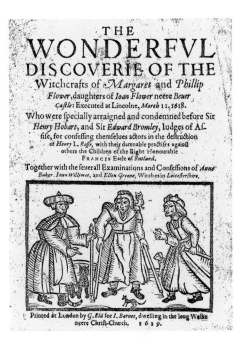

(known in the play as Meg) sing a rollicking little ditty to Mamilion: "Then suck our blouds freely, and with it be jolly, / While merrily we sing, hey Trolly Lolly." Tap your toes in time to the jaunty rhyming verse as Frances Dickenson plots to turn herself and her demonic side-kick, or "puckling," into dogs, just as Edmond Robinson had pictured her: "I and my puckling will a brace / of Greyhounds be, fit for the race." Cheer and clap as she leads her unholy cohorts in a rustic witches' dance.

The women from Lancashire were guilty as sin—of that, the play left no doubt. ("We represent [only] as much / As they have done," the authors assured the crowd.) But instead of recoiling from the witches in horror as their neighbors back home had done, the smart set in London felt free to make a savage joke of them. For what were these women, when all was said and done, but a bunch of silly old wives and country bumpkins?

Meanwhile, behind closed doors at the law courts, the story was being replayed again, though this time in an appropriately somber context. The jeering laughter of the theater mob faded to a hush of learned talk among the black-robed officials of the Privy Council. Yet even here, the reality of witchcraft was not openly in doubt. Witchcraft was against the law, therefore it had to exist: otherwise the whole judicial system would be brought into disrepute. But what did pubicly concern the judges were matters of proof. In these most problematic of cases, how could the courts be certain they were getting at the truth?

There were still plenty of judges around who followed Pierre de

No appeal was launched in the case of the Flowers of Beuer Castle, who were hanged in 1618 *The Huntington Library, San Marino, California*

Lancre's lead and pandered to the lowest form of credulity. But a new spirit was rising—in London as nowhere else—that demanded a more rigorous approach to gathering evidence. According to the proponents of the new science, the only sure road to the truth was the careful study of observable facts. This revolutionary method had recently proven its worth in the work of the king's own physician, the great William Harvey, who in 1628 had overturned centuries of error with his discovery of the circulatory system. Now Dr. Harvey was summoned by the court to study the Lancashire "witches" and scientifically reassess their alleged witch marks.

Leaving nothing to chance, Dr. Harvey assembled a team of seven surgeons and ten certified midwives to conduct the examination. Their verdict contradicted the findings of the Lancashire court: the supposed witch marks were nothing but natural skin blemishes, piles and warts. In the absence of concrete evidence, the whole case soon fell apart. Poor witless Granny Johnson proved unable to keep her story straight. Frances Dickenson, finally given a chance to speak in her own defense, charged that the accusation against her had been an act of petty vengeance engineered by Edmond Robinson's father—an assertion that was subsequently supported by other witnesses. As one official noted, it was hard to get the facts clear, because the village had been a hornets' nest of deceit and malice.

It was left to little Edmond to bring the proceedings to a close. Separated from his father, he finally told the truth. There hadn't been any witches' feast; he had merely stopped to play and had made up his story to avoid being beaten for coming home late. His evidence had

Dr. Harvey and the Toad

Once upon a time—or so it is said—William Harvey visited the city of Newmarket in eastern England. There he heard of a supposed witch who lived in "a lone house on the borders of a Heath." He decided to pay her a call, and though the woman greeted him with mistrust, he won her cooperation by introducing himself as a fellow magician. At this, she let him into her confidence.

What he really wanted, Harvey said, was to see her "familiar," or demonic pet, which she called on to help her work her spells. (The familiar was a special feature of English witchcraft—a magical assistant in the form of a boy or small animal.) Obligingly, the woman brought out a saucer of milk and made a chuckling noise, like the murmuring of a toad. Sure enough, from under a chest, out hopped the woman's toad to take a drink.

Now that Harvey had seen her familiar, he needed the woman to leave, so he suggested that she should set out and get them some ale to drink. No sooner was she out of the house than the doctor seized the toad and slit it open. After examining it closely, he decided that the small corpse in his hand was an ordinary amphibian. Far from being a demon, it had simply been the pet of lonely and delusional old woman.

When the woman returned and found her familiar was dead, she flew at her visitor "like a Tigris." Unable to calm the woman with explanations or gifts, Harvey turned menacing. He was the king's physician, he said, and if her toad had lived, he could have had her charged with witchcraft. At that, the woman released him from her grip, and the doctor quickly fled.

Background: A witch feeds her toad-like familiars.
From A Rehearsall both straung and true of Hainous and Horrible Acts Committed by Elizabeth Stile, *1579, British Library,* STC 23267

By the end of the eighteenth century, the witch would be fitted out in her complete party-time kit: haggard face, black cape, buckle shoes and broomstick. The type of the Halloween witch had already been set.

been "false and feigned," he admitted now, without any "truth at all, but only as he ha[d] heard tales and reports made by women, so he framed the tale out of his own invention." The whole affair had rested on nothing more than gossip, poisoned by village intrigue, compounded by incompetent rural officials and confirmed by a credulous jury of small-town hicks. Case dismissed.

At this point we hope for a triumphant conclusion in which the women are returned to their homes, with compensation for their troubles and apologies from everyone involved. Instead, a complete anticlimax—nothing happens at all. A full three years later, in the fall of 1637, five of the surviving "witches" are still being held in a cold, dark, barren room in Lancaster Castle; many of the others have already died in jail. Although the courts had cleared the women of guilt, the country still cried for their blood, so the judges had taken the easy way out and left them to rot in prison. Who cared, anyway? For who were these women, when all was said and done, but a bunch of silly old wives and country bumpkins?

The tragic case of the Lancashire witches did not mark the end, nor even the beginning of the end, of witch prosecutions in Great Britain. Another hundred years would pass before, in 1736, the crime of witchcraft was finally stricken from the books and, without so much as a "poof!", the Devil-worshipping witch officially ceased to exist. By the end of the eighteenth century, the witch craze had pretty much fizzled out both in Europe and in America. Yet before that had happened, the face of the witch had already started to shift and blur, as she was re-envisaged by a new generation of skeptical spin doctors.

From the shadows of doubt and confusion that had hung over the trials, a creepy new image of the witch was beginning to emerge.

A figure of pathos and ridicule, this new witch was Granny Johnson writ large—a foolish old village woman awash in dreams and impossible tales. Incompetent in the courtroom, she was a natural on the stage and soon became a favorite at stylish masquerades. We meet her, for example, at a fancy-dress party held in Windsor in 1724, where one gentleman amused the company by donning an apron and the tall pointy hat of an old-fashioned country woman. By the end of the eighteenth century, the witch would be fitted out in her complete partytime kit: haggard face, black cape, buckle shoes and broomstick. The type of the Halloween witch had already been set.

Tens of thousands of women and men had died appalling deaths, and this was the way their suffering was to be commemorated.

Yet this teasing, half-mocking image of the witch had been conceived with a generous purpose in mind. The mission was to quench the flames and save innocent lives. The most direct way of ending the panic—exposing the witch as a fiction and the Devil as a fraud—was, for the moment, thoroughly blocked. The Scriptures said that both were real, and that was the end of that. Even in the bold new age of reason and science, no one but a reckless fool would dispute the word of God. As John Wesley put it in 1768, "The giving up of witchcraft is, in effect, giving up on the Bible," something that, at the time, was still beyond the pale. Besides, if witches did not exist, then who had been killed, and why? These were treacherous questions and best set aside.

Yet as the educated classes of the Enlightenment increasingly

As her supposed victims swoon and faint, lower right, an accused witch is examined for blemishes that testify to her liaison with Satan. It was common for midwives and other knowledgeable women to be called into court to provide expert testimony on witch marks. *Examination of a Witch* was painted by T. H. Matteson in 1853, based on events in New England in the 1690s.

Peabody Essex Museum, Salem, MA

"THE GUILT OF INNOCENT BLOOD"

The infamous witch trials in Salem Village (now Danvers), Massachusetts in 1692 number among the sorriest events in American history. Fourteen women and five men were convicted of witchcraft and hanged—despite their pleas of innocence. In addition, an old beggar woman named Sarah Good died in jail, and a man named Giles Corey was literally pressed to death for refusing to cooperate with the prosecution. As many as a hundred other people were held in prison for months, unsure of the terrors that might await them.

Witch belief had crossed the Atlantic with the settlers, and the trials at Salem were closely based on precedents in England. The panic began when two little girls began having terrible fits, and the local doctors concluded that they had been bewitched. Soon other girls began to thrash about as if they too were possessed, and adults joined in the unholy chorus. (A woman named Sarah Viber claimed that the "Apperishtion" of Sarah Good had choked, beaten, pinched and pricked her with pins "after a most dreadfull manner.") The case against the female suspects was duly confirmed by the discovery of witch teats on their skin.

It was only after the hangings that the community began to recoil from what it had done. Shortly thereafter, the jury took the unusual step of apologizing for having brought "the Guilt of Innocent Blood" upon the people of Salem. The prisons were emptied, and in 1710, the Massachusetts government offered partial compensation to accused witches and their descendants.

"There is a flock of yellow birds above her head." This dramatic reconstruction of the Salem courtroom appeared in *Harper's New Monthly Magazine* in 1892.
Peabody Essex Museum, Salem, MA

transferred their faith to the new scientific approach, their doubts about witchcraft continued to grow. Toothless old women who flew through the night? Humans who turned into hares? People who were seen in two places at once on the Devil's errands? For the unlettered folk in the villages these tales still glowed hot with truth, but for the bigwigs in the city, the embers were cooling to ash. The experts started to look for a way to get the soot off their hands.

The trick was to bring the witch-craze to an end without drawing shame on themselves or provoking a crisis of confidence in the entire system. And what better way to do this than by blaming the victims instead. For, like young Edmond Robinson, the learned folk still knew what witches were for: when you were in trouble, they gave you someone to blame. There would never have been a witch-craze, the scholars now proclaimed, if it had not been for the foolish—even demented—talk of ignorant women out in the country.

Forget the learned ravings of Kramer and Sprenger. The blood-thirsty certainty of Pierre de Lancre. The calm efficiency of a Lancashire court that had sentenced seventeen people to death. Think no more of the thousands of pages of closely reasoned witch-theory that, over the centuries, had spilled from the pens of lawyers and theologians. The lists of prescribed questions. The instructions to torturers. The esoteric arguments about demonic sex. Suddenly, none of this scholarly outpouring had the slightest importance. The whole episode had been the fault of the common people, whose minds, as it now appeared, were susceptible not only to superstition but also to mental illness.

This jolly little Halloween witch appears blissfully unaware of her distressing ancestry. *David and Michele Hargis*

Background: Witches in steeple-crowned hats often appeared in eighteenth-century pamphlets and chapbooks. *Peabody Essex Museum, Salem, MA*

"By witches, the common people understand those who have the power to fly through the air at night-time to remote places where they worship the Devil and abandon themselves to intemperance and lust," an eighteenth-century French encyclopedia sneered. "This is in fact a baseless illusion: the so-called 'witches' sabbath' is a disease of the imagination . . . [a conclusion that] is proved by unquestionable experience."

The poor old souls who confessed to being witches had actually been quite mad. Like the ancient followers of Diana who had believed in their flying dreams, they had been misled by their diseased imaginings. Far from being agents of Satan, these women were just what they seemed: feeble and weak-minded old nobodies. To proceed against such people in court was as illegal as it was cruel. For as the Reverend Francis Hutchinson had argued in 1718: "Courts of Justice

The Order of the Holy and Undivided Trinity of Castle Rising, in Norfolk, England, was founded in 1610 as a refuge for impoverished old women. They look like witches to us because the witch-figure had been made over to look like an old-fashioned country woman. *Library of Congress, LC-USZ62-95578*

fINISHED BUSINESS

Bible-thumping churchmen continued to promote the belief in witchcraft well into the eighteenth century. But despite their best efforts, the passion for witch-hunting was spent. The Devil-worshipping witch was a thing of the past, a relic that had outlived its usefulness.

The witch had once stood as the emblem of sin and disorder—of everything that was wrong with the common people. But in the sixteenth and seventeenth centuries, a new moral discipline had been imposed by the missionaries, and a spirit of penitence and restraint had settled upon western Europe. In the course of a few generations, the people had been reformed. For the first time in European history, they began to question their own basic desires. In Puritan England, for example, the rate of illegitimate births dropped by as much as three-quarters.

Women were especially constrained by the moral reforms, which placed their ambitions under tight control. According to the new vision, women were made for marriage and, to that end, their education was now increasingly geared toward domestic accomplishments. In countries ruled by Protestant monarchs, convents were closed, and women lost their only chance of a general education. Debarred from studying Latin, the language of scholarship, they were prevented from participating in the development of the new science. To justify this exclusion, women were now told that they were naturally irrational and overemotional.

As science became ever more powerful in the eighteenth century, women's knowledge was increasingly pushed aside. This was particularly true in the medical field, where university-trained (male) doctors rapidly gained ground from female midwives and village healers. The victory against "white witches" was thus eventually achieved by bloodless regulation and bureaucracy.

The History of the Devil by Daniel Defoe was published in 1815 as a last-ditch attempt to resurrect the belief in diabolical witchcraft. Happily, it did not achieve its goal, but it did feed the growing taste for fantastical stories and the occult.

British Library, 1490B31

66 ✦ Witch

may as well hang People, upon their Confessions, for the Murders they think they commit in their Dreams," as for what a supposed witch fancies she does in her reveries. So what if a madwoman came to believe she had signed a pact with Satan and "joyned with other Witches in Murders, and confessed them? What wise Man would have turned such a Confession to her Hurt? Physick for Madness would be proper for such a one; but a Stake, or Gallows, would be barbarous."

If witches were nothing but "brainsick" old crones, the legal case against them could no longer stand. Instead of submitting these poor souls to the judgment of the church and the law, they should be put in the care of a good doctor. Someone perhaps like Dr. Harvey himself, who had written with such authority about women's mental health. Like most medical men of his age, Harvey shared the traditional view that women's minds were inherently unstable because of the peculiar nature of the uterus. Unlike all other human organs, which were fixed in place, the womb was credited with the unique ability to roam around at will, like a restless animal inside the body's walls. One day it might be down by the liver, the next month up near the throat. "No one of the least experience can be ignorant what grievous symptoms arise when the uterus either rises up or falls down, or is in any way put out of place, or is seized with spasm!" the great doctor pointed out. Among the alarming consequences of these dislocations were psychological symptoms—the "mental aberrations, the delirium, the melancholy, the paroxysms of frenzy, as if the affected person were under the dominion of spells." Yet, thankfully, science had now shown that these problems were the natural result of more-

or-less routine uterine displacements. Similar disturbances might also occur in women who failed to menstruate or got too little sex, facts that put older women and widows at special risk. Small wonder, from a scientific point of view, that this group had been so tragically prone to the delusions of witchcraft.

In one respect at least, Kramer and Sprenger had clearly been right. Women became witches (whether in fact or fantasy) because they had wombs. But instead of propeling women into the clutches of Satan, as the witch-haters had maintained, the womb now stood accused of plunging women into the grip of insanity. While a man might pass through life in

The agonies of demonic possession were depicted in a painting entitled *The Trial of George Jacob, August 25, 1692* by the American artist T. H. Matteson. *Peabody Essex Museum, Salem, MA*

the sure light of reason, women were naturally given to superstition, confusion and violent passion, all the result of their physiological weakness. As one contemporary expert on mental disorders was good enough to explain, "Women, from any sudden terror and great sadness, fall into mighty disorder of spirits, where men from the same occasion are scarcely disturb'd at all." Madness (like witchcraft before it) had now been defined as the special province of womankind.

The link between witchcraft and mental illness seemed particularly apt in accounting for the bizarre spectacle of "demonic possession." These cases typically began when the subject, often a young woman or a teenage girl, became convinced that she had been invaded by an evil presence. Her symptoms (duly documented by her attending physicians and clergymen) were strange and disconcerting. Her body was tortured by spasms; she vomited needles and pins. Alien voices came out of her mouth and made rude and shocking statements. Often, the malady spread to the girl's sisters or friends, who began to develop similar manifestations. Sooner or later, someone would suggest that the "demoniacs" had all been bewitched—that is, that the devils had been imposed on them by a local witch.

That was exactly what happened in Würzburg, Germany, in 1745. The "victims" in this instance were a group of nuns, who suddenly began to complain that someone was trying to suffocate them. That

By the nineteenth century, the fits and spasms of hysteria had been classified as a disease of the nervous system. Here, the renowned Dr. Jean-Martin Charcot uses one of his patients to demonstrate the phases of an hysterical seizure. *Jean-Loup Charmet*

Utter Bedlam

In the 1600s and 1700s, treatment for insanity was a queasy mixture of kindness and cruelty. While a well-to-do woman might be able to find a humane doctor, a poor old "witch" was likely to be shut up in the howling squalor of a public institution—someplace like the Hospital of St. Mary of Bethlehem in London (the original Bedlam) or its sister institution, La Salpêtrière, in Paris.

In her memoirs, Louise du Tranchay wrote of her confinement in La Salpêtrière in 1674. For the entertainment of visitors, she and the other inmates were put on public display, caged and chained like beasts. Visitors were permitted to make the women howl by poking their walking sticks through the bars.

By the nineteenth century, La Salpêtrière had evolved into a respected center for research into the perplexing disorder of "hysteria" (from the Greek *hystera*, or womb), the disease that had been blamed for the trance-like states, delusions and fits of witchmania. At La Salpêtrière, these symptoms were treated, without much success, with cold baths, electric shock and a new-fangled torture device called an ovarian compres-

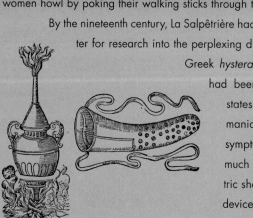

In the iconography of witchcraft, the strange forward movement of the hair had been used as a sign of the Devil's unnatural powers. In 1811, the same symptom reappeared in a scientific text on hysteria. *Bibliothèque nationale de France*

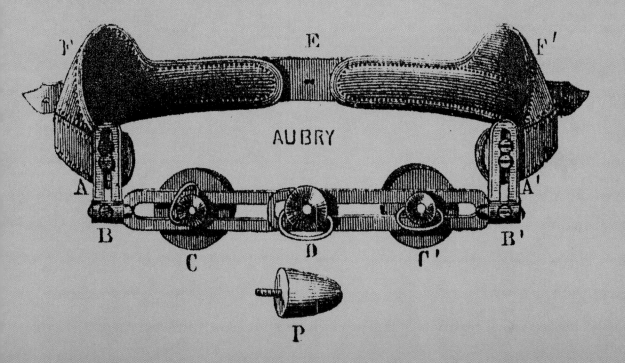

AUBRY

sor. Other treatments came straight out of the witch-hunters' book—pricking the victim with bodkins to study insensitive spots or shearing off the patient's hair as a therapeutic shock.

In the 1870s, La Salpêtrière was especially famous for the Tuesday morning sessions at which head researcher Jean-Martin Charcot displayed his understanding of hysteria. Using hypnotized patients as models, Charcot would illustrate the classic postures of a hysterical fit, which he said were the result of damage to specific nerves. In time it became clear that these symptoms were actually being produced by suggestible and well-trained patients, at the doctor's behest, to validate his theory and observations.

The mystery of hysteria was eventually "solved" by a one-time student of Charcot's named Sigmund Freud. As he saw it, the disorder was the physical manifestation of unconscious memories and repressed desires, which were "converted" into bodily symptoms. Fits were no longer important in diagnosing the disease, and by the early 1900s these dramatic symptoms had all but vanished.

Instead of using an ovarian compressor like the one pictured above, some nineteeth-century physicians preferred to surgically remove the ovaries of their hysterical patients. Earlier, doctors had attempted to lure the wandering uterus back into place by fumigating it with the device shown on the facing page. *Florence Collection*

someone, they said, could only have been one of their fellow sisters, a young woman named Maria Renata Sänger. The afflicted nuns swore that she haunted their bedrooms in the form of a pig or a cat, and suckled cows out in the meadows as a bewitched rabbit. Despite the advances of science, Maria was burned alive, but she would, thankfully, be one of the last to die. A few decades later, when a similar scare broke out in Quebec, church officials refused to intervene. The fits of the supposed "demoniac" had natural causes, they said, and should be treated by doctors.

The common folk didn't always take kindly to this withdrawal of official support. For them, the presence of demons and witches remained as fearful as ever. When the authorities refused to take action, people sometimes sought vengeance for themselves, even to the point of lynching suspected witches. Yet vigilante justice now carried its own dreadful price. When Ruth Osborne of Hertfordshire, England, was killed by a mob of her neighbors in 1751, a man named Thomas Colley was promptly arrested, tried for her murder and hanged. Under these circumstances, witch-hunting quickly lost its attractions.

The fear of witchcraft would continue to haunt the people of some remote, rural districts of western Europe for another hundred years and more. But the wildfire of panic had finally been put out. By 1756, a lawyer in the Vaud district of Switzerland—the very region in which the witch crisis had started three centuries before—could look back on the atrocities with nostalgic calm. "Witches were burned in former times," he said. "Today, there aren't any." For once people of all social classes had begun to withdraw their belief, the Devil-wielding witch

had miraculously vanished. In her place there now stood an antic, half-crazed old hag with a broomstick and black cat. By shifting the idea of the witch onto less dangerous ground, this silly old soul had done her job. Fact had morphed into fairy tale, fear into fascination, and the whole atmosphere had been perceptibly brightened. Yet despite these transformations, this new witch was still cursed with shame—the legacy of the witch craze would not pass away in a day.

ROMANCING the Witch

Since we [women] have been banished
from the country of reason and knowledge,
and left with nothing but the empire of the imagination,
it is at least necessary to dream nobly.

The Marquise de Lambert, 1711

We have come to a border crossing. Behind us lie the smoldering ruins of the Kingdom of Darkness, where so much blood has been shed. Ahead we see a signpost, *"Bienvenue dans le monde des fées"* (Welcome to Fairyland).

It is fitting that we should encounter this greeting first in French, since that is the language in which the wonders and terrors of the fairy realm were about to be described in print. Many of our all-time favorite fairy tales—including "Cinderella," "Puss in Boots" and "Beauty and the Beast"—were initially published in France, just at the time when the witch craze was coming to an end. And this timing was by no means a coincidence.

By the end of the seventeenth century, educated people knew as a matter of common sense that women were naturally irrational. And this applied not just to the "witches" and "demoniacs" who were now locked up in asylums, but to all women everywhere. Unlike men, who stood on the firm ground of reason and fact, women groped their way through a shadowy realm of feelings and dreams. They had a childlike taste for fantasy (or so the experts said) and an innate affinity with the old peasant world of witchcraft and magic. Although folk stories and superstitions were beneath the notice of any

Facing page: The magical fairy land of Arthur Rackham is full of witch-like figures. Here, an apple tree shelters a sweet-faced girl from an evil crone. *de Grummond Children's Literature Collection, University of Southern Mississippi*

Below: Cinderella's magical fairy godmother tumbles down the chimney to her rescue. *Florence Collection*

75

rational male, they had a naive, unstudied charm that made them especially suitable for the weaker sex.

What the experts did not anticipate was that fairyland would quickly become a clandestine site for women's self-expression. Yet this is exactly what happened, and one of the people we have to thank was a writer—and schemer—by the name of Marie-Catherine d'Aulnoy. Born to an aristocratic family in Normandy around 1650, she was married off to a repulsive old man at the age of fifteen, and it was this calamitous marriage that first led her to become engaged in the excitement of intrigue. In 1669, she and her mother, with their respective lovers in tow, spread rumors that her husband had criticized the king, an offense that carried the death penalty. But Monsieur d'Aulnoy turned the tables on their plot and sent the women's hapless lovers to the block. Mother and daughter escaped into exile and spent the best part of twenty years skulking about western Europe, eventually (it was

Guests at the ball in Rackham's *Cinderella* might easily pass for a gathering of women at Madame d'Aulnoy's salon. *Florence Collection*

said) working as secret agents for the French government.

In 1685, Marie-Catherine d'Aulnoy was allowed to return to Paris, where she established herself as the center of a "literary salon"—a kind of perpetual come-and-go tea that featured ladies, and some gentlemen, in an endless round of brilliant conversation. Here, she found herself surrounded by women after her own heart: irreverent, smart, ambitious and utterly devious. One of her closest friends went to the guillotine for killing her abusive husband (a plot in which Madame d'Aulnoy was rumored to have had a hand). And members of her circle were almost certainly involved in the sensational scandal of *l'affaire des poisons*. The last large-scale witch trial in France—and one of the strangest—the case had centered on a network of abortionists and poisoners who, into the 1680s, had catered to the special needs of upper-class Parisian ladies. Dozens of high-ranking women had found themselves hauled into court to answer charges of abortion, infanticide and conspiracy to commit murder. When the investigations reached into the bedroom of the king, the prosecutions were suspended abruptly.

But nothing could stem the passionate outpourings of women's talk that swirled through the corridors of Madame d'Aulnoy's salon. Such laughter. Such wit. Such charm. Such carefully concealed venom. Yet

By the late seventeenth century, members of the aristocracy had begun to dabble, ever so stylishly, in witchcraft and the occult. This painting of an unnamed French noblewoman is entitled *The Witch. Jean-Loup Charmet*

despite their clandestine rage, the salonistes were not in total revolt against the conventions of their age. They did not, for example, appear to take offense at the continual, learned put-downs of the female sex. If women were said to be irrational, emotional and impulsive, the salonistes were quite prepared to accept these statements as read. If that was what women were like, they'd play the role to the hilt, dazzling the world with their marvelous flights of fancy and their tenderness. They also prided themselves on their womanly talent for love—though few of them found it with their husbands.

And here lay the heart and soul of their grievances. Virtually to a woman, the salonistes had been forced into marriage without their consent, pawns in what were essentially financial transactions between wealthy men. All too often, as in the case of Madame d'Aulnoy, the outcome had been miserable. So what the salonistes yearned for was the freedom to choose for themselves—to follow desire wherever it led. But desire, especially the wanton urgings of the female heart, had long been said to run inevitably, irrevocably towards Satan. (Although women could no longer be tried as witches, they could still be scorned as whores.) By demanding a measure of sexual liberty, the salonistes now found they had entered the lists against a resurgent moral-reform movement. The God Squad was out to get them.

Their chief opponent in this battle was Louis XIV's new wife, a droopy-eyed, pursed-lipped moralist named Madame de Maintenon. In the wake of *l'affaire des poisons*, Madame had taken a determined and public stand against virtually everything the salonistes represented. Women were to serve their husbands, she wrote, not run around look-

Facing page: In the so-called *affaire des poisons*, a group of high-ranking French noblewomen employed the services of a Parisian sorceress-cum-abortionist named Catherine La Voisin, as a way of covering up their extramarital liaisons. The seventeenth-century artist Jacob de Gheyn seems to have anticipated just such an event in his view of a witches' kitchen.
Bildarchiv Preussischer Kulturbesitz, photo by Jörg P. Anders, Staatliche Museen, Berlin

ing for love. To submit. To seek seclusion in their homes. To cherish duty. To cultivate silence, so "suitable to the sex." For the sake of their souls, for the sake of their children, for the greater glory of France, she called on them to forsake worldly distractions and take up the womanly cross of keeping house. "Irreproachable behavior," Madame de Maintenon said, "is [every woman's] greatest accomplishment."

The salonistes answered this challenge in the way that they knew best: with wit, laughter and evasiveness. Well aware that open resistance would draw the ire of the king, they were nevertheless determined to make their case. Just suppose, they began to muse wistfully, that there once had been a world in which the grim code of the moralists had never been heard. A world in which the pursuit of true love was a woman's highest goal. Where there was no God and no Devil—

no Madame de Maintenon—and no one had ever been burned for witchcraft. "Once upon a time," Madame d'Aulnoy began . . .

Night after night, Madame d'Aulnoy and her friends (mostly ladies, but also a few men) entertained each with other wild, improbable tales of a magical fairyland in which female power held the upper hand. In the late seventeenth century, these beguiling fantasies began to appear in print, including a four-volume set of *Fairy Tales* from Madame d'Aulnoy herself. The "literary fairy tale," as the new genre became known, immediately took the reading public by storm. Dozens of volumes were rushed into print, including Charles Perrault's stylish and much-loved collection, *Tales From Mother Goose.*

In creating their splendid adventures, the fairy-tale writers drew on whatever sources lay close at hand, including the literary classics. (Thus the romance *Cupid and Psyche* by the second-century Roman author Apuleius provided the theme for countless renditions of "Beauty and the Beast.") But the salonistes went out of their way to obscure this high-minded heritage. Rather than hinting at a serious purpose, it seemed wiser to pretend that they were just creating a harmless entertainment. So they claimed to have found their inspiration exclusively in the folktales they had heard in their youth, from their nursemaids and other members of the lower class. Their stories were just silly "old wives' tales," or so they hoped people would think, and of no possible interest to the authorities.

By casting their fiction in the form of folktales (however fake), the

The early fairy-tale writers invited their readers to believe that their stories came straight from the untutored mouths of their servants. This is the frontispiece from the first English edition of Charles Perrault's *Tales From Mother Goose,* published in 1729.
Florence Collection

BEWITCHING MOTHER GOOSE

As the author of the well-known versions of "Cinderella," "Sleeping Beauty" and "Little Red Riding Hood," Charles Perrault (1628–1703) is one of the most influential of modern writers. Yet he is not exactly a household name, and that is at least in part because he did his level best to keep from being one.

At the time he published his fairy tales, Perrault was engaged in a heated, public debate over the direction that French literature should take. Should writers draw their inspiration from the classics of Greece and Rome or find their inspiration in modern culture? After a decade of listening to arguments sawing back and forth, the king weighed in on the side of the classicists. But as a determined modernist, Perrault still wanted to have his say, and that is why he published his skilfully edited folktales. By providing the stories with morals, he hoped to show that literature could be created from even the most "lowly" of materials.

Aware of the risk he was taking in talking back to the king, Perrault needed distance himself from his stories. He did this by inventing the persona of Mother Goose and making it appear as if she (and not he) was the original storyteller. Who could be offended by the fancies of a sweet-faced old granny?

In succeeding centuries, Mother Goose would, of course, take on a life of her own, as an emblem of fun and fantasy for children. In the warm glow of firelight around her rocking chair, she spun her tales of pure imagination. Here nothing was to be feared, not even the wicked witches who began to appear in nineteenth-century children's literature. By then, the witch was so much at home in the kingdom of Mother Goose that she had taken on a striking resemblance to her hostess. The witch on her broomstick and Mother on her goose were pictured as flights of fancy—just the thing to lull tiny tots to sleep.

The salonistes tried to disguise their subversive intentions by "clothing" themselves in the foolish fancies of the lower class. (This evil fairy, in her elaborate gown and old-fashioned peasant hat, comes from the pen of Arthur Rackham.)

de Grummond Children's Literature Collection, University of Southern Mississippi

salonistes were able to slip their thoughts past the noses of the censors. The old magical beliefs—with their shapeshifters, familiars and fiends—had fallen into such disrepute that no eighteenth-century thinker could bring himself to consider them seriously. Even the cultivated women who took shelter in their midst were sometimes inclined to wonder if they'd covered themselves in filth. "I think," one of the salonistes wrote disdainfully, "that these Tales were filled with impurities by passing through the mouths of lowly people, just as pure water is laden with garbage when it passes through a dirty gutter."

Although they appropriated folk motifs and used them in their work, they had no interest in conserving the stories in their traditional form. Instead, the salonistes blended folk ideas into more-or-less original stories in which female beings—not entirely unlike themselves—occupied the spotlight as both heroes and villains.

The protagonists in these escapades were typically princesses and queens who overcame seemingly impossible odds to win the men of their dreams. Almost without exception, they were assisted in their quest by some kind of a wonder-working fairy guardian. Against them there usually stood a bad-tempered fairy or an ogress: a monstrous mother-in-law in the original version of "Sleeping Beauty," an evil fairy named Magotine in Madame d'Aulnoy's tale "The Green Serpent," and a fairy lioness in her "The Beneficent Frog." Yet never once do these early literary fairy tales feature the figure of the witch, with her animal familiars and her flying broomstick. Even as a fiction, the witch still represented the view that a woman who stepped out of bounds was irretrievably damned. In their effort to make room for themselves and their forbidden desires, the salonistes banished this possibility from their fantasy realm. In their pages, the worst that could be said of any female—whether of human or fairy stock—was that she was angry, vengeful and miserably unpleasant. Female "evil" had been brought within the compass of normal human response, free from even the slightest trace of fire and brimstone. Speaking in the coded language of their fiction, the salonistes thus became the first female writers to take a stand against the legacy of the witch hunt.

Erasing the witch was a strategy, a sly gesture of dissent against the

Facing page: By the nineteenth century, Mother Goose and the fairy-tale witch had taken on a shared identity. In this illustration from *Dame Dearlove's Ditties for the Nursery* (1830), for example, the good old Dame can scarcely be distinguished from a witch or evil fairy. The two figures were united by their common status as foolish old grannies who entertained children. Their distinctive facial features were borrowed from yet another comical old crone—the ignorant village woman who was the butt of many a joke in pantomime. *Osborne Collection of Early Children's Books, Toronto Public Library*

THE GREEN SERPENT

Of all Madame d'Aulnoy's fairy tales, one of the few that remains in print is the racy and extravagant saga of *"Le serpentin vert"* (*"The Green Serpent"*). First published in 1698 within the context of a novel, the story traces the misfortunes of the princess Hildessa, who has fallen under the curse of "the most wicked fairy" in existence. Magotine, as she is known, is a short, ugly grouch who commands a company of marionettes and an army of insects. Jealous at being excluded from the celebration of Hildessa's birth, Magotine has turned the princess into the ugliest creature on Earth.

In her grief at her deformities, Hildessa retreats to the Lonely Castle, where she passes her time playing instruments and writing books. One day she encounters a creature as ugly as herself—a dreadful green serpent who scares her half to death. But soon the serpent saves her from a mysterious shipwreck, and she finds herself magically transported to his luxurious estate. There, cloaked in invisibility, the gentle beast wins her love, though he insists she must not see him until seven years are up. He too is under a curse of the evil Magotine, and they both will pay a terrible price if Hildessa ignores this warning.

Inevitably, the foolish Hildessa sneaks a premature peek, and she and the poor serpent are condemned to misery. Magotine then sets the princess a series of impossible tasks, such as spinning spider's silk and visiting the underworld. But with the help of Guardian Fairy, Hildessa breaks the spell, and she and the serpent-prince are restored to their original loveliness. For "whatever Magotine's powers, alas for her," Madame d'Aulnoy concludes, "what could she do against the power of Love?"

In one of Madame d'Aulnoy's tales, the black-hearted fairy-villain used her magic wand to turn the heroine's companions into griffons.
Roger-Viollet

brutal judgments of the moralists. But, sadly, the salonistes' resistance had been doomed from the start; they had never really stood a chance against Madame de Maintenon and the forces of moral reform. Yet, while the brilliant society of the salonistes faded from the scene, their tales remained on the best-seller lists until almost the end of the eighteenth century. Printed in inexpensive editions and distributed far and wide, they spread their seditious, underground gospel—with nary a witch in sight.

But the evil old biddy was still standing in the wings, waiting for the cue that would bring her back into the thick of things. Her moment would come early in the nineteenth century, when a group of scholars suddenly got in a rush to collect the vanishing wisdom of the common folk. (This was the same "wisdom" that had previously been held in scorn as superstition, "lowly" trash and heretical error.) Leading the lineup of researchers were the German brothers Jacob and Wilhelm Grimm, whose famous collection, *Nursery and Household Tales*, was first published around 1815. Although little more than a hundred years had passed since the heyday of the salonistes, the world had changed and changed again. Revolutions in America and in France had toppled kings from their thrones and created a wave of enthusiasm for the Noble Common Man. Even as this was

Rapid industrialization in the nineteenth century created a belated appreciation for the knowledge and belief of simple people out in the country.

Dover Pictorial Archive

happening, common people by the thousands were being ignobly forced to leave their farms and villages to work in factories. To people like the Brothers Grimm who were distressed by these trends, the old peasant beliefs and stories now carried the nostalgic scent of fresh-mown hay and honest sweat.

As pioneers of the new science of "folklore" (so new the term hadn't been coined), the Grimms espoused the revolutionary view that the old peasant tales were laden with ancient truths. These stories were not merely mementos of times gone by, they said; instead, they were frag-ments of wisdom from the earliest stages of human development. Rather than thinking of the stories as (say) pebbles that had been shaped by historical change, the brothers described them as little gems that had come through the flood unscathed.

If the stories were universal and timeless, as the Brothers Grimm said, then one version of a tale was as valid as the next; there was no need to fuss about "authentic" sources. So most of the stories in their collection came to them not from gnarly old peasants but from family friends, notably a handful of middle-class women. Well versed in the oral tradi-tion, these informants were also well read in the wondrous *faux* folktales of the salonistes, and elements from the written accounts crept into their storytelling. The Grimms' version of "Cinderella," for example, was true to its age-old roots except for the inclusion of the glass slipper, a device that had been added around 1700 by the French writer Charles Perrault. This idea hadn't come from the soul of the *volk* at all. And, if anyone had cared to think about it, questions might also have been raised about the figure of the wicked witch that appeared in a few of the

Background: Cinderella displays her rags to her fairy godmother in this illustration by Arthur Rackham. *Florence Collection*

tales. Was she really a spontaneous invention of the primeval folk, or had she been
dreamed up more recently, at the time the
witch hunt?

These kinds of subtleties were of no
real interest to the Brothers Grimm or to their first generation of readers. Instead of castigating the brothers for straying too far from the
genuine source, their contemporaries were more inclined to berate
them for getting too close to the unwholesome roughness of the common people. They were especially incensed by the thought that the
Grimms presented their tales as a collection of "nursery" stories to be
told to young children. Although publishing for children was still relatively new, the public's expectations were emphatic and clear. Books
for young people should be moral and uplifting, never vulgar or crude.
Judged by this standard, the Brothers Grimm had failed miserably.
One reviewer likened their book to a suit of dirty clothes, with miss-
ing buttons and dangling shirt-tails; another dismissed it brusquely as
"real junk."

In response to these complaints, Wilhelm Grimm immediately set
to work on a revised (and hopefully more saleable) edition of the
book. One issue that especially called for his attention was the
instruction of little girls—the wives and mothers of the future. As
adults, these girl children would be called to a life of womanly virtue
and self-sacrifice. Yet there was Cinderella, in the original edition of
the book, boldly speaking for herself and asking to try on the glass
slipper! With a quick stroke of his pen, Grimm took the words out of

In an attempt to improve
sales of their book, the
Grimms made their
heroines increasingly
passive. By the time they
were finished, the only
females in their tales who
had any spark were the
witchy villains. When
Walt Disney came upon
the Grimms' work more
than a hundred years
afterwards, he was
inspired by their example.
His animated fairy tales
invite girls to choose
between two role models:
the witch and the sweet
young thing. *British Film
Institute/© Disney Enterprises, Inc.*

The specter of the witch craze, which the salonistes had exorcized with their wit, had returned to haunt the pages of the Brothers Grimm. As ever, the witch stood as a warning of the evil that women could do if they ever dared to stray away from "family values."

her mouth and forced her to wait demurely for her prince to come. And as poor Cinderella became more insipid, her wicked rivals became just the reverse: more talkative, more aggressive, more vindictive—and more accursed. Subtly, silently, the witch was creeping back into the frame to embody the fears of the Brothers Grimm and their contemporaries.

The revisions to "Hansel and Gretel" took this impulse to the extreme. In the original transcript, the story begins with an impoverished woodcutter who has "fared so miserably" that he is unable to feed his wife and family. Faced with imminent starvation, the wife then proposes that they lead their two children into the forest, give them all the remaining bread and abandon them to fend for themselves. The father regretfully accepts the suggestion. But by the fifth edition, of 1843, the father has been absolved of all wrongdoing. "Great need [had arisen] in the land," Wilhelm Grimm explains, and the poor man clearly could not be held to blame. What's more, the mother—by now a stepmother—is made to propose that they leave the children with only a crust of bread, presumably in the hope that they will starve to death. The father tosses and turns with worry and professes his reluctance, but he cannot withstand the persuasions of the evil stepmother. Thus, an act of brutal necessity has been neatly transformed into a black-hearted travesty of womanly nature.

Meanwhile, out in the dark forest, "the small old woman" with her house of bread and cake has been transposed into a "wicked witch" with a taste for children's flesh. "If one got into her power, she killed it, cooked it, and ate it," the fifth edition elaborates with glee, "and that was for her a day to celebrate." When Gretel kills the witch (by now with the aid of prayer), Grimm goes to great lengths to make the villain suffer. "Whoo! Then she began to howl, quite horribly," he writes, but Gretel runs off and leaves the "godless witch" to die wretchedly in the fire. When the children return home, they find their stepmother too is dead. The abusive mother and the terrible witch cannot be separated.

The specter of the witch craze, which the salonistes had exorcized with their wit, had returned to haunt the pages of the Brothers Grimm. As ever, the witch stood as a warning of the evil that women could do if they ever dared to stray away from "family values." Women were meant to be nurturers, to be docile, loving and sweet; the only other option was to be a witch/bitch. Unlike the French fairy-tale writers, whose villains were each unique (there was nobody else quite like the nasty Magotine!), the Brothers Grimm drew all their female monsters with the same heavy hand. Cruel stepmothers, evil fairies, enchantresses and queens all merged into one forbidding figure of maternal hostility. The darkest power in fairyland, in the eyes of the Brothers Grimm, was the witchy resentment of a Bad Mother.

This new conception of the witch was an immediate hit in an age

A monstrous witch, designed by Louis Rhead in 1917, orders Gretel to climb into the oven to see if it is hot. *Osborne Collection of Early Children's Books, Toronto Public Library*

Horror Stories

By the nineteenth century, most people agreed that the witch was just a harmless fantasy. Yet even as fiction, she could still be used to express a deep—and deeply troubling—ambivalence towards women.

The Brothers Grimm, for example, redrew the figure of the witch as a monster of maternal vengeance. Even though women were believed to be motherly at heart, they evidently could still be seduced by the dark powers of jealousy and resentment. The Grimms' extravagantly evil female villains stood as suggestive evidence that women, as mothers, were not to be trusted. The hand that rocked the cradle could ruin the world if women's witchy emotions were not kept under control.

At about the same time as the Grimms began their work, a young English novelist was following along a parallel thematic track. His name was Matthew Lewis, and in 1795 he created a sensation with his Gothic novel *The Monk*, which explored the dangers posed by women as sexual temptations. Set at the time of the Spanish Inquisition, his story traces the downfall of Ambrosio and his seduction by the luscious young Matilda. Although Ambrosio does not know it, Matilda is a witch, and her powers of fascination are literally Satanic. Under her malign influence, he pursues a career of gynocide and rape—though it is not entirely clear if he is to blame. Does the fault reside with him or with Matilda, the treacherous *femme fatale* who had lured him away from the straight and narrow? To this day, the idea that women "bewitch" men into assaulting them is still sometimes heard as an excuse for sexual violence.

Kay Nielsen's stunning depiction of Rapunzel and the witch dates from 1925. *Osborne Collection of Early Children's Books, Toronto Public Library*

that insisted on motherhood as women's rightful domain. Yet in doctoring their material, the Grimms apparently had no sense that they were rewriting the tales to suit their era and themselves. Instead, they thought they were merely adding little touches—filling in the gaps—so that the age-old insights of the folk could be more easily grasped. Despite all the evidence of tampering (by other hands as well as their own), they continued to insist that the stories were fragments of primitive scripture—"remains of an ancient faith extending far back into the oldest times"—truths transmitted by word of mouth from the childhood of humankind. Thus, the Witch Mother now took her place among the age-old human myths, as if the fears of the nineteenth-century middle class were themselves timeless.

If the cruelty of mothers was humankind's primal fear, then women were clearly called upon to be exquisitely tender. In the lacy parlance of Victorian advice manuals, wives were exhorted to see themselves as "angels of the house"—saints of the nursery—who found the entire meaning of life in their maternal duties. Motherhood should be the sole wish of every woman, her complete preoccupation, with no room for business or public life or self-expression. Any woman who pursued "outside" interests was abandoning her children to the wolves, as surely as if she were one of the Grimms' evil stepmothers.

Although a century or more had passed since the last witch had been burned, women were, in a very real sense, still being held pris-

More liberty for women meant less for men. At least, that was the fear of social conservatives. *Library of Congress, LC-USZ62-40599*

Below: The only power a "true woman" could want was the power of mother love. *Dover Pictorial Archive*

oner. An entire sex had been detained in their homes and held there by force of law, barred from participating in politics, the universities or the professions. And any time they tried to break out—by demanding the vote, for example, or access to birth control—they were scolded for being Bad Mothers and told to go back home.

By the late nineteenth century, a band of renegade women had strengthened their resolve and decided to fight for women's rights, whatever it might cost. Among this determined sisterhood was a tiny, bright-eyed Englishwoman by the name of Margaret Murray, who was destined to give the Grimms' wicked witch a run for her money. Like the salonistes before her, Murray would elaborate a new myth in which women who followed their hearts' desires emerged as heroines. Through the magic of creative scholarship, the witch was about to be transformed into a standard-bearer of the women's cause.

Born in 1863—the year of Jacob Grimm's death—Murray encountered the study of folklore where the brothers had left it. Like them, she shared the conviction that folktales provided a link with the primeval religious traditions of the human race. After persisting unchanged through all the earliest ages and stages of Man, this Old Religion had ultimately been quashed by the intrusion of the Christians. Beginning in 1890, this seductively simple theory was given its definitive form in the twelve successive volumes of James Frazer's *The Golden Bough*. By assembling selected titbits from the mythologies of the world, Frazer constructed a persuasive picture of an age-old fertility cult, which he presented authoritatively as humankind's primal religion.

By the 1920s, when Frazer's research was complete, Margaret

Background: For Margaret Murray, as for James Frazer, the strange beliefs of the past were imbued with meaning for the present. *Dover Pictorial Archive*

Murray had established herself as an authority in the study of ancient beliefs. Unable to enroll at university because of her sex, she had pursued her interests informally and made a name for herself as an interpreter of Egyptian hieroglyphics. But when this research was interrupted by the First World War, she turned her attention to a cryptic puzzle that lay closer to home. Someone had once suggested to her that the witches of the "middle ages" might have been followers of an

Margaret Murray, second from the right, unwraps a mummy, 1908. A pioneering anthropologist, she was one of the first scholars to study the documents from the witch trials.

Romancing the Witch ✦ 93

THE WITCH GOES GLAM

In their love affair with rationality, Enlightenment thinkers like William Harvey had thrown the subject of witchcraft into the cultural trash. But by the end of the eighteenth century, the sun of reason had begun to set amidst the moody, moonlit skies of the Romantic movement. A radically new generation with revolution in their bones, the Romantics were infatuated with everything that their forefathers had disowned. For them, dreams and imagination were the essence of humankind; they provided a link with the Eternal, a connection to the Divine. Surely, they thought, reality

was something more than a cold structure of logic and facts; it was numinous, magical, suffused with spirit. If Dr. Harvey had believed that he could grasp the truth by slicing up an old woman's toad, the Romantics believed that mystery was to be savored as a whole.

The essence of mystery for the Romantic movement was captured by the female sex and—especially—by the image of the witch. Instead of seeing the witch as a witless old crone, the Romantics brought her into view as the Eternal Feminine, the

Above: Frederick Sandys's *Medea* casts a seductive spell. *Birmingham Art Gallery*
Right: Rita Hayworth in a Hollywood photo.
Motion Picture magazine

sorceress and muse who held mere males under her spell. As one writer put it in 1896, "We have banished the broom and the cat and the working of miracles, the Sabbat and pacts with Satan, but the mystery or puzzle is as great as ever. . . . [T]o this day—as most novels bear witness—it is recognized that there is something uncanny, mysterious, and incomprehensible in woman, which neither she herself nor man can explain. . . . Are not the charms of love of every kind, and the enjoyment of beauty in all its forms in nature, mysteries, miracles, or magical?"

"For every woman," he concluded, "is at heart a witch." But unlike Pierre de Lancre, who had harbored the same thought, the Romantics insisted they meant this as a compliment!

Margaret Murray was not the only scholar to write about the survival of a fertility cult. French historian Jules Michelet had advanced a similar view in 1862. But unlike Murray, who gave women a starring role in the old religion, Michelet thought they had sometimes served as objects of worship. *Jean-Loup Charmet*

Background: This updated conception of the witches' god appeared in a nineteenth-century manuscript on the occult. *Dover Pictorial Archive*

ancient cult since, like some of Frazer's primitives, "they had danced round a black goat." With this thought in mind, she now began to rummage through the documents that survived from witch craze, including transcripts of the Lancashire trials and the writings of Pierre de Lancre.

By her own account, she set to work with the still "usual" view that the witches were tragic old wives who had been trapped in a net of lies and delusions. But it didn't take long for her to break through this conventional under-standing to a deeper—and more startling—level of meaning. With a sudden burst of comprehension, she real-ized that the supposed Devil of the witchcraft trials was really a flesh-and-blood man, who had played the part of the god in an ancient nature religion. When the "Devil" appeared in animal form, it was this same figure in disguise, maintaining a religious tradition that stretched back to the cave art of paleolithic times. The witches had been practi-tioners of an age-old pagan cult, which they sustained in proud defi-ance of the Christian church. "The numbers of the witches put to death by the inquisitors and other persecutors in the 16th and 17th centuries" now stood as dreadful "proof" of Margaret Murray's stunning new nar-rative.

Sylvain, god of the forest, was one of hundreds of deities that had once been venerated by the peoples of western Europe. Margaret Murray claimed that a horned god had been the focus of the witch cult. *Bibliothèque nationale de France*

Yet what readers could not know at the time was that Murray had cooked the books, by committing scholarly crimes of both commission and omission.

When she'd happened upon a titbit she liked, she had made the most of it, disguising her lack of evidence with a tone of calm assurance.

Murray laid her case before the public in 1921 in a dry-as-dust anthropological treatise called *The Witch-Cult in Western Europe*. Surely nothing this meticulous and boring could possibly be mistaken. In page after detailed page, she quoted snippets from hundreds of trials to build up a composite picture of the witches' fertility rites. Virtually every statement she made was supported, chapter and verse, with examples drawn verbatim from the original trial records. Yet what readers could not know at the time was that Murray had cooked the books, by committing scholarly crimes of both commission and omission. When she'd happened upon a titbit she liked, she had made the most of it, disguising her lack of evidence with a tone of calm assurance. (For example, she made the sweeping assertion that witches met in covens of thirteen on the basis of a single piece of trial testimony.) Conversely, details that didn't suit her views were ignored without comment, on the grounds that they had been introduced by hostile witnesses.

Take, for example, the insistence—so central to the trial transcripts—that the witches had worked harmful spells against their neighbors. Balderdash, said Murray; is that how a priestess would act? The accusations against the witches were scarcely worth mentioning, so permeated were they with distortions and misunderstanding. Since the women belonged to a fertility cult, the church had darkly assumed that they had the power to work anti-fertility charms. (Hence, the suspicion that they had caused abortions and impotence.) The fact that their opponents had raised these charges was now reconstrued as proof that the witches had actually done the exact opposite. Far from

TRICK OR TREAT

Thanks to Margaret Murray, we all now "know" that witches met in covens of thirteen members. And this is not her only contribution to popular witch lore. By picking and choosing her sources, she was also able to "prove" that the witches observed four major Sabbaths a year, joyful celebrations with much singing and dancing that, she said, were held on February 2, May-eve, August 1 and, of course, November-eve—better known to us these days as Halloween.

Unfortunately for Murray's theory of a universal pre-Christian cult, her four festivals do not seem to have been widely observed in western Europe. Instead, they were originally confined to Ireland and Scotland alone, as elements of a specifically Gaelic culture. At least, that is the conclusion of historian Ronald Hutton, in his recent and respected books on the pagan religions of ancient Britain.

As Hutton tells the story, the pagans of western Europe did not follow a standardized calendar. Instead, festivals differed from region to region and, in time, were overwritten by equally varied Christian customs. In the case of Halloween, for example, he locates one point of origin in the Gaelic festival of Sawhain, which was celebrated on November 1 to mark a moment when spirits and goblins wandered the earth. By the early Middle Ages, this occasion had been merged with an eerie Christian festival of the dead, which originated in England and Germany around AD 800. Customs from both traditions live on in the present-day celebration of Halloween—the dress-up comes from the pagans and the door-to-door visitations began as a Christian custom of "begging bread for the souls of the dead." The modern festival of Halloween developed in the United States in the early 1900s and, from there, has been exported to other parts of the world.

Halloween postcards were exchanged between friends in the early 1900s.
David and Michele Hargis

being the Anti-Mother, Murray began to hint, the witch had been a shining light of motherly love.

Murray's audacious fantasy was a block-buster success and established her as the leading expert on European witchcraft. (From 1929 onwards—for the next forty years—her views would reign as fact in the leather-bound pages of the *Encyclopaedia Britannica.*) Buoyed by this endorsement, she threw caution to the winds and elaborated her theory with enthusiasm. If the wickedness of the witches had been in the eyes of their enemies, then Murray would make it her mission to restore their beauty. "For centuries both before and after the Christian era," Murray now claimed, "the witch [had been] both honoured and loved" by all her friends and neighbors in the village. Despite the disapproval of the church, she had been consulted by everyone "for relief in sickness, for counsel in trouble, or for fore-knowing of . . . coming events." She had been a rebel, a healer, a priestess, a seer, in touch with the spirit of the universe. The shade of Granny Johnson had been conjured back to life as a figure of splendor and light.

Like the Brothers Grimm before her, Murray had set out to reveal the truth that lay hidden in a collection of folkloric fragments. But where the Grimms had encountered the specter of female malevolence, Murray had found a wondrous fount of womanly inspiration. Like the salonistes before her, she had answered myth with myth. If Madame d'Aulnoy could only have known, she would have been tickled pink.

Facing page: For women of Murray's generation, the joyful fantasy of the witch religion offered a "memory" of a golden age of liberty. Evelyn De Morgan expressed her longing for freedom in a 1919 painting called *The Gilded Cage. De Morgan Foundation/Bridgeman Art Library. Above: Dover Pictorial Archive*

BROOMSTICK RIDE.

LITTLE boys, and little girls,
  Will you come and ride;
On my pretty broomstick,
  Flying far and wide.

First around the blazing Sun,
  And then around the Moon;
And then around the steeple,
  To hear a merry tune.

LIFTING the Curse

Tremble, tremble, the witches have returned!
Tremate, tremate, le streghe son tornate!

Chant from a feminist demonstration, Italy, 1970s

Margaret Murray had it wrong; of that there is now little doubt. The people who died as witches in the sixteenth and seventeenth centuries were not members of an underground pagan cult, much less one that met in covens, celebrated Celtic holy days or worshipped the god Dianus—the "age-old" deity that Murray dreamed up for them. We can point out her errors with confidence, thanks to the meticulous work of a new generation of historical researchers. A legion of academics have been rummaging through the archives for the last twenty or thirty years, re-reading the same strange, hallucinatory old records to which Murray had referred. But although the scholars continue to squabble about exactly what it all means, they are in agreement about one thing. They can find no convincing evidence for an organized witch cult of any sort, whether dedicated to Dianus, or to Diana, or to the Devil.

The vibrant religion that Murray described almost certainly did not exist, and its defiant priestesses were little more than wistful illusions. Like a photographer in a darkroom, she had taken the negative image of the diabolical witch and, by reading black as white, transformed it into a figure of beauty and light. Murray's life-affirming priestesses had no more standing in fact than the Devil-worshipping viragos that they had displaced.

Facing page: Despite the cheerful jingle of her words, Kate Greenaway's gruesome-looking witch has not quite escaped from the shadows of her difficult past. de Grummond Children's Literature Collection, University of Southern Mississippi. Below: Byzantium Archive

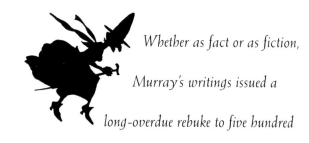

Whether as fact or as fiction,

Murray's writings issued a

long-overdue rebuke to five hundred

years of woman-bashing

and abuse.

But as the story of the witch craze has repeatedly shown, an idea does not have to be correct to be important. Whether as fact or as fiction, Murray's writings issued a long-overdue rebuke to five hundred years of woman-bashing and abuse. First, she rejected the idea that the witch persecutions had been caused by the superstitions and delusions of "brainsick" old crones. (It had been "unscientific," she objected, "to label all the phenomena [reported at the trials] as the imagination of hysterical women.") And if the "witches" themselves were not to blame, then suspicion must naturally turn towards their judges and prosecutors. The perversions of the witch craze had been the result, Murray said, of the distorted and hate-filled ideas of powerful men.

For some right-wing Christians, the horrors of witchcraft are as real and present as ever. *Kerr and Malley, anti-abortion demonstrators, Los Angeles, 1989*

DO THE UNDEAD DEMONS OF HELL STILL ARISE TO TERRORIZE THE WORLD?

AMERICAN INTERNATIONAL PRESENTS

BURN WITCH BURN

JANET BLAIR · PETER WYNGARDE · MARGARET JOHNSON · produced by ALBERT FENN
screenplay by RICHARD MATHESON and CHARLES BEAUMONT · directed by SIDNEY HAYERS · A JULIAN WINTLE - LESLIE PARKYN PRODUCTION · AN AMERICAN INTERNATIONAL PIC

Right on, sister! By the 1960s (around the time of Murray's death, at the ripe old age of one hundred), a generation of defiant young feminists had hit the streets to protest against the distorted and hate-filled ideas that still jeopardized their sex. "Whatever is repressive, solely male-oriented, greedy, puritanical, authoritarian—those are your targets," declared a leaflet published by a women's liberation group in New York City on Halloween of 1968. To mark this festive occasion, the activists signed themselves as WITCH—the Women's International Terrorist Conspiracy from Hell. This name, they said, marked their awareness that the witches of history had been "the original guerillas and resistance fighters against oppression—particularly the oppression of women—down through the ages." If witches had stood in sisterhood against The Man, as the *Encyclopaedia Britannica* still suggested, then they had been the advance guard of the women's movement.

The witch was chosen as a revolutionary image for women, WITCH's Chicago coven confirmed, because witches had struggled long and hard against their patriarchal oppressors.

In a story that is full of striking ironies and unexpected twists, this is surely one of the weirdest. For it is a tragedy of history that the witch hunt demonstrably *failed* to provoke any significant resistance among the common people. Instead, both women and men were panicked into collaborating with their persecutors, unable to withstand the persuasions of pulpit-thumping and brute force. The individuals

If women were getting uppity out on the streets, they could still be punished on the silver screen. *Burn, Witch, Burn* was released in North America in 1961, as part of a Gothic revival that would eventually include such blockbusters as *Rosemary's Baby* (1968), *The Exorcist* (1973) and *Carrie* (1976). *American International Pictures*

who were accused of witchcraft faced the terror alone, with little scope for resistance except sometimes—heroically—by saying no. "I do plead not guilty." "I can deny it to my dying day." "I am Innocent as the childe unborne." "God knows I am innocent." "I am no witch." Yet, a few centuries later, these isolated voices would be recalled as a triumphant "memory" of solidarity and collective struggle. The anguish of the accused witches has been persuasively transformed into a source of inspiration for their great-great-great-great-great-great-great-great-granddaughters.

This resplendent vision—of women standing together against the forces of repression and death—lies at the heart of Wicca, or feminist witchcraft. At first glance, an attempt to "revive" a subversive religious movement that didn't ever exist may not seem to have much going for it. But New Age witches have risen above the embarrassment of their

Today, many Wiccans trace the origins of their faith to the great monuments of the Stone Age. It seems that every successive redefinition of witchcraft has projected its origins farther back into the past. *Jean-Loup Charmet*

dubious ancestry. With a wave of their intellectual magic wands, they have transformed Murray's vision of the past into a hopeful and challenging theology for the present.

Murray described her witches as devotees of a male demon or god, because that was how they had been described in the trial records. But she was aware that certain scholars (notably the mythographer Bachofen) believed that Europeans had originally venerated a female divinity. Extrapolating from this theory, Murray noted that her witch cult, in the far distant past, had likely been devoted to a great Mother Goddess. This is a possibility that Wicca has taken enthusiastically to heart by invoking a panoply of female deities, from the Egyptian Isis—last heard from around AD 400—to the sumptuous Sumerian Inanna, Queen of Heaven and Earth, whose rites have not been practiced for the past four thousand years. On the eve of the twenty-first century, witchcraft has been reborn as the faith of the "timeless" Goddess in her many forms.

But despite its claims to antiquity, Wicca also takes its stand unashamedly in the here and now. "Although Goddess religion is unimaginably old," one of its leading exponents explains, "contemporary Witchcraft could just as accurately be called the New Religion.

In their hunger for female divinity, Wiccans have adopted goddesses from a wide range of cultural traditions. *Dover Pictorial Archive*

The Craft, today, is undergoing more than a revival, it is experiencing a renaissance. . . . Women are spurring this renewal, and actively reawakening the Goddess, the image of 'the legitimacy and beneficence of female power.'"

The moral stance of Wicca has been most eloquently expressed by a down-to-earth Californian with an infectious grin who has taken the spirit-name of Starhawk. Born in 1951 as Miriam Simos, she was raised as a Jew and remembers herself as a "very religious" little girl. Yet "as I reached young womanhood in the late sixties, something seemed lacking." That something turned out to be an immanent female deity, present in each stone and blade of grass, alive in the flesh and blood of every person. "The importance of the Goddess symbol for women [in particular] cannot be overstressed," writes Starhawk in her influential guidebook, *The Spiral Dance.* (Subtitled *A Rebirth of the Ancient Religion of the Great Goddess,* it was first published in 1979 and quickly became a classic of the feminist spirituality movement.) "The image of the Goddess inspires women to see ourselves as divine, our bodies as sacred, the changing phases of our lives as holy." There is nothing evil about women, she reminds us, nor has there ever been; we are exactly who we were meant to be.

For serious practitioners of Wicca, magic is not something that can be bought in a vial at the corner shoppe. Instead, in the words of Starhawk, it is the profound art of "bending the unseen into new forms." By "unseen" she means the unconscious beliefs and images that we have inherited from the past. In practicing magic—even by play-

In 1899, Charles Leland produced a book entitled *Aradia: The Gospel of the Witches,* which he said had been dictated to him by a surviving member of the witch cult—pictured above. *Florence Collection*

fully casting a spell—"we speak to the unconscious in the symbolic language it under-
stands." The objects and images used in spells
"communicate directly with [the unconscious,
or] Younger Self, who is the seat of our emotions and who is barely touched by the intel-
lect." In this way, "we attain the most important
power—the power to change ourselves."

It is this possibility of deep, transformative
change that lies at the heart of feminist witchcraft—change not only for individuals but also
for the culture as a whole. As some Wiccans
see it, the world today is threatened by the
same malevolent spirit of domination that
caused the witch craze. The devaluation of
women has implied a devaluation of life, and

A lively young witch
smiles out at us from a
Halloween postcard.

Florence Collection

western culture literally needs to be revitalized. "Whether our immediate needs are for food, health care, jobs, childcare, housing, or open
spaces, our ultimate interest is the same—restoring a sense of the
sacred to the world, and so restoring value to our own lives and to the
community of beings—human, plant and animal—that share life with
us." This is a rich moral palette that runs through the entire spectrum
of political resistance, from feminism and gay liberation to pacifism,
conservation and social justice. The witch has cast aside her broomstick and donned the shining robes of the High Priestess of cultural
renewal.

We have come a long way from the blood-thirsty rantings of the *Malleus Maleficarum*. Between the hatred of Kramer and Sprenger and the affirmations of the Wiccans lies a gulf of error and incomprehension. The women who were killed as witches had remarkably little in common with the women who choose to carry the name in the present. Yet their experiences are nonetheless linked by the tortuous narrative that we have traced, round many a hairpin bend, in the preceding chapters. In our transit through the centuries, we have watched as the specter of the female witch first coalesced in the prurient theories of theologians and judges in the Renaissance. We saw how this apparition was subsequently invoked by the Bible-thumping preachers of the Reformation. Under their vociferous persuasion, village people came to believe that Satanic evil was walking their streets. This fear—directed mostly against older women—fanned the flames of panic.

As the killing slowly came to an end in the mid-seventeenth century, the witch was recast as a mentally unstable old granny. Soon the whole idea of witchcraft shifted—hat, cat, broomstick and all—into the realm of childish fiction. But even decked out as a figure of fancy and fun, the witch continued her subtle campaign against women. On the one hand, she represented the notion that women were prone to madness and foolish fantasies, and hence ought not to be taken seriously. On the other, the witch could still stand as a warning of the evil that women could do if they strayed too far from the straight and narrow. As the Brothers Grimm reminded us through their dark editorializing, powerful, ambitious women are downright scary.

Facing page: In the 1960s and 70s—just as the women's movement was beginning to stir the pot—*Bewitched* poked gentle fun at women's desire for power. But as poor Darrin discovered to his rue, there was little that a mere man could do. *Columbia TriStar Television*

Background: Bewitched's Samantha followed in the tradition of Arthur Rackham's magical fairy godmothers. *Florence Collection*

Pages 112–13: "When he went over the wall, he was terrified to see the witch before him." *Arthur Rackham, The Fairy Tales of the Brothers Grimm, 1909, Osborne Collection of Early Children's Books, Toronto Public Library*

Once upon a time, back in the seventeenth century, the salonistes had tried to limit the witch's dangerous career simply by refusing to acknowledge her. But, as their experience ultimately proved, the witch will not go away just because we want her to. Margaret Murray and the Wiccans have tried another tack, by reimagining darkness as light. Yet they too have fallen under the evil old spell by focusing on women's supposed gifts for intuition, enchantment and nurturance. Even in its most positive incarnation, the figure of the witch still represents the view that women are uncanny, exotic—not quite human.

More than five hundred years after the first witch flew off a printed page, she continues to haunt our minds, from our first childhood encounter with Disney to our latest cinematic excursion into the shadowy backwoods of Blair township. Perhaps the witch's continuing presence is a sign that, collectively, we still fear the untrameled expression of women's desires. Until that unease is magically laid to rest, the witch will continue her wild ride into the future.

Lifting the Curse ✦. 113

NOTES

Notes refer to direct quotations only. For a more complete listing of sources, please consult the References.

vii Roald Dahl, *Roald Dahl's Revolting Rhymes* (New York: Alfred A. Knopf, 1982), p. 1.

SECRETS OF A SHAPESHIFTER

1 Horace Walpole, as quoted by Anne Williams, *Art of Darkness: A Poetics of Gothic* (Chicago: University of Chicago Press, 1995), p. 27.
"Generation Hex," from Alexandra Gill, "Girls Just Wanna Have Wands," *Globe & Mail*, 29 May 1999, sec. C, p. 1.

2 Trial of Gratiosa, as quoted by Guido Ruggiero, *The Boundaries of Eros: Sex, Crime and Sexuality in Renaissance Venice* (Oxford: Oxford University Press, 1985), p. 34.

CONJURING A NIGHTMARE

11 Ecclesiasticus XXV, as quoted in Heinrich Kramer and James Sprenger, *Malleus Maleficarum*, translated and edited by Montague Summers (1928; reprint, New York: Dover, 1971), p. 43.
Re fascinating eyes: Pierre de Lancre, *Tableau de l'inconstance des mauvais anges et démons*, 1612, as quoted by Gerhild Scholz Williams, *Defining Dominion: The Discourses of Magic and Witchcraft in Early Modern France and Germany* (Ann Arbor: University of Michigan Press, 1995), p. 111.
Re woman thinking alone, natural temptation: Kramer and Sprenger, *Malleus Maleficarum*, p. 43.

13 Michel de Montaigne, "On Cripples," as quoted by Jeffrey B. Russell, *A History of Witchcraft: Sorcerers, Heretics, and Pagans*

(London: Thames and Hudson, 1981), p. 73.

17 de Lancre, *Tableau*, as quoted by Rossell Hope Robbins, *The Encyclopedia of Witchcraft and Demonology* (New York: Crown Publishers, 1974), p. 41.

24 Roman law code, as quoted by Kurt Seligmann, *The History of Magic* (New York: Quality Paperback Book Club, 1997), p. 113.

26 Charlemagne's law codes, as quoted by Ilza Veith, *Hysteria: The History of a Disease* (Chicago: University of Chicago Press, 1966), p. 57.

27 Regino of Prüm, *De Ecclesiasticis Disciplinis II*, as quoted by Valerie I. J. Flint, *The Rise of Magic in Early Medieval Europe* (Princeton: Princeton University Press, 1991), p. 122.

28 Re dreams and nightmares: Burchard of Worms, *Corrector*, as quoted by Flint, *The Rise of Magic in Early Medieval Europe*, p. 123.

30 Geoffrey Chaucer, "The Wife of Bath's Tale," in *The Works of Geoffrey Chaucer*, edited by F. N. Robinson (Boston: Houghton Mifflin, 1957), p. 84.
Palermo fisherman's wife, as quoted by Gustav Henningsen, "'The Ladies from Outside': An Archaic Pattern of the Witches' Sabbath," in *Early Modern European Witchcraft: Centres and Peripheries*, edited by Bengt Ankarloo and Gustav Henningsen (Oxford: Clarendon Press, 1990), pp. 196–97.

32 Re frailty of women: Kramer and Sprenger, *Malleus Maleficarum*, pp. 41, 42, 44.

34 Re carnal lust: Kramer and Sprenger, *Malleus Maleficarum*, p. 47.

36 Re senility: Bishop of Innsbruck, as quoted by Wolfgang Behringer, "Witchcraft Studies in Austria, Germany and Switzerland," in *Witchcraft in Early Modern Europe: Studies in Culture and Belief*, edited by Jonathan Barry et al. (Cambridge: Cambridge University Press, 1996), p. 83.

Re the end of the world: Kramer and Sprenger, *Malleus Maleficarum*, p. 16.

40 Re white witches: William Perkins, *A Discourse of the Damned Art of Witchcraft* (1608), as quoted by Keith Thomas, *Religion and the Decline of Magic* (New York: Charles Scribner's Sons, 1972), p. 177.

Martin Luther, *The Table Talk of Martin Luther*, as quoted in *Witchcraft in Europe 1100–1700: A Documentary History*, edited by Alan C. Kors and Edward Peters (Philadelphia: University of Pennsylvania Press, 1972), p. 195.

42 Charms, as quoted by K. M. Briggs, *Pale Hecate's Team: An Examination of the Beliefs on Witchcraft and Magic among Shakespeare's Contemporaries and His Immediate Successors* (London: Routledge and Kegan Paul, 1962), pp. 170–73, 184.

43 Martin Luther, 1531, as quoted by Lyndal Roper, *Oedipus and the Devil: Witchcraft, Sexuality and Religion in Early Modern Europe* (London: Routledge, 1994), p. 19.

John Knox, *The First Blast of the Trumpet against the Monstrous Regiment of Women*, 1558, as quoted by Selma R. Williams, *Riding the Nightmare: Women and Witchcraft from the Old World to Colonial Salem* (New York: Harper, 1992), p. 65.

OLD WIVES' TALES

45 Squire Henry Oxiden of Kent, as quoted by James Sharpe, *Instruments of Darkness: Witchcraft in England 1550–1750* (London: Hamish Hamilton, 1966), p. 56.

Re characteristics of witches: John Baule, 1646, as quoted by Frances E. Dolan, *Dangerous Familiars: Representations of Domestic Crime in England, 1550–1700* (Ithaca: Cornell University Press, 1994), p. 88.

46 Margaret Johnson, as quoted by Diane Purkiss, *The Witch in*

History: Early Modern and Twentieth-Century Representations (London: Routledge, 1996), p. 237.

49 Re witches' mark: from the court records, as quoted by Laird H. Barber, *An Edition of "The Late Lancashire Witches" by Thomas Heywood and Richard Brome* (New York: Garland, 1979), p. 65.

52 Edmond Robinson's statement, as quoted by John Webster, *The Displaying of Supposed Witchcraft* (London: J. M., 1677), p. 362. Source: http://www.witchcraft.psmedia.com.

54 Description of pamphlets and plays, as quoted by Barber, *"The Late Lancashire Witches,"* p. 73.

55 Speeches by the stage witches, as quoted by Barber, *"The Late Lancashire Witches,"* p. 152 (Act II, scene i).

"We represent," as quoted by Barber, *"The Late Lancashire Witches,"* p. 217 (Epilogue).

57 The story of William Harvey and the toad is based on a letter, purportedly written by a justice of the peace in south-western England in 1685 and first published in *Gentleman's Magazine* in 1832. It is quoted by Wallace Notestein, *A History of Witchcraft in England from 1558 to 1718* (1911; reprint, New York: Russell & Russell, 1965), p. 161.

58 Edmond Robinson's retraction, as quoted by Sharpe, *Instruments of Darkness*, p. 164.

59 John Wesley, from his journal, 1768, as quoted by Herbert Leventhal, *In the Shadow of the Enlightenment: Occultism and Renaissance Science in Eighteenth-Century America* (New York: New York University Press, 1976), p. 66.

62 Sarah Viber, from documents on display at the Peabody Essex Museum, Salem, Massachusetts.

Apology of the Salem jury, as quoted by Francis Hutchinson, *An Historical Essay Concerning Witchcraft*, 1720, p. 138. Source: http://www.witchcraft.psmedia.com.

64   French encyclopedia, *Encyclopédie méthodique*, 1790, as quoted by Julio Caro Baroja, "Witchcraft and Catholic Theology," in *Early Modern European Witchcraft: Centres and Peripheries*, edited by Bengt Ankarloo and Gustav Henningsen (Oxford: Clarendon Press, 1990), p. 42.
      Reverend Francis Hutchinson, *An Historical Essay Concerning Witchcraft*, as quoted by Ilza Veith, *Hysteria: The History of a Disease* (Chicago: University of Chicago Press, 1966), p. 73.
      William Harvey, *On Parturition*, as quoted by Veith, *Hysteria*, p. 130.

69   Re women's instability: contemporary expert Thomas Willis, *An Essay on the Pathology of the Brain and Nervous Stock in which Convulsive Diseases are Treated of*, 1684, as quoted by Veith, *Hysteria*, p. 133.

72   Lawyer in the Vaud, as quoted by E. William Monter, *Witchcraft in France and Switzerland: The Borderlands during the Reformation* (Ithaca, N.Y.: Cornell University Press, 1976), p. 40.

ROMANCING THE WITCH

75   The Marquise de Lambert, as quoted by Lewis C. Seifert, *Fairy Tales, Sexuality and Gender in France 1690–1715: Nostalgic Utopias* (Cambridge: Cambridge University Press, 1996), p. 247. The Marquise de Lambert was actually an opponent of fairy tales and the novel, which she found tasteless.

79   Madame de Maintenon, as quoted or paraphrased by Nancy Mitford, *The Sun King* (London: Hamish Hamilton, 1966), pp. 167, 122.

82   Mademoiselle Marie-Jeanne L'Héritier, 1696, as quoted by Seifert, *Fairy Tales*, p. 66.

84   "The Great Green Worm," by Marie-Catherine d'Aulnoy, translated by A. S. Byatt, in *Wonder Tales: Six Stories of Enchantment*, edited by Marina Warner (London: Vintage, 1996), pp. 211, 227.

87   Grimms' critics, as quoted by Maria Tatar, *The Hard Facts of the Grimms' Fairy Tales* (Princeton: Princeton University Press, 1987), p. 16.

88   Successive editions of "Hansel and Gretel," from John M. Ellis, *One Fairy Story Too Many: The Brothers Grimm and Their Tales* (Chicago: University of Chicago Press, 1983), pp. 176–94.

91   Re "Ancient truths": Jacob Grimm and Wilhelm Grimm, as quoted by Jacqueline Simpson, *European Mythology* (New York: Peter Bedrick Books, 1987), p. 12.

95   Re the mystery of womanhood: Charles G. Leland, *Aradia: The Gospel of the Witches* (1899; reprint, London: C.W. Daniel, 1974), p. 114. Although supposedly dictated to Leland by an Italian witch, *Aradia* was a fabrication.

97   Re the black goat: Margaret Murray, *My First Hundred Years* (London: William Kimber, 1963), p. 104.
      Re witches put to death: M. A. M. [Margaret Alice Murray], "Witchcraft," *Encyclopaedia Britannica* 23 (1929, 14th edition): 687.

99   "Begging Bread," as quoted by Ronald Hutton, *The Stations of the Sun: A History of the Ritual Year in Britain* (Oxford: Oxford University Press, 1997), p. 374.

101   Re witches as honored and loved: Margaret Murray, *The God of the Witches*, 1933, as quoted by Jacqueline Simpson, "Margaret Murray: Who Believed Her, and Why?" *Folklore* 105 (1994): 93.

LIFTING THE CURSE

103   Chant, as quoted by Silvia Bovenschen, "The Contemporary Witch, the Historical Witch and the Witch Myth: The

Witch, Subject of the Appropriation of Nature and Object of the Domination of Nature," *New German Critique* 15 (fall 1978): 83.

104   Margaret A. Murray, *The Witch-Cult in Western Europe: A Study in Anthropology* (1921; reprint, Oxford: Oxford University Press, 1962), p. 177.

105   WITCH Pamphlet, as reprinted in *Sisterhood Is Powerful: An Anthology of Writings from the Women's Liberation Movement*, edited by Robin Morgan (New York: Vintage, 1970), pp. 539–40.

106   "I do plead not guilty," etc., from the witch-trial memorial at Salem, Massachusetts.

107   Re New Religion: Starhawk, *The Spiral Dance: A Rebirth of the Ancient Religion of the Great Goddess* (1979; reprint, San Francisco: Harper and Row, 1989), p. 23.

108   Re something lacking: Starhawk, *The Spiral Dance*, p. 2.
        Re the Goddess symbol: Starhawk, *The Spiral Dance*, p. 24.

109   Re the power to change one's self: Starhawk, *The Spiral Dance*, p. 125.
        Re restoring value: Starhawk, *Dreaming the Dark: Magic, Sex and Politics* (1982; reprint, Boston: Beacon, 1988), p. 219.

REFERENCES

SECRETS OF A SHAPESHIFTER

The Witch Craze in Europe: An Overview

Barry, Jonathan, et al., eds. *Witchcraft in Early Modern Europe: Studies in Culture and Belief.* Cambridge: Cambridge University Press, 1996.

Barstow, Anne Llewellyn. *Witchcraze: A New History of the European Witch Hunts.* San Francisco: Pandora, 1994.

Briggs, Robin. *Witches and Neighbors: The Social and Cultural Context of European Witchcraft.* New York: Viking, 1996.

Klaits, Joseph. *Servants of Satan: The Age of the Witch Hunts.* Bloomington: Indiana University Press, 1985.

Levack, Brian P. *The Witch-Hunt in Early Modern Europe.* London: Longman, 1987.

Muchembled, Robert, ed. *Magie et sorcellerie en Europe du moyen age à nos jours.* Paris: Armand Colin, 1994.

Ruggiero, Guido. *The Boundaries of Eros: Sex, Crime and Sexuality in Renaissance Venice.* Oxford: Oxford University Press, 1985.

Ryan, W. F. "The Witchcraft Hysteria in Early Modern Europe: Was Russia an Exception?" *SEER* 76 (1998): 49–84.

Whitney, Elspeth. "The Witch 'She'/The Historian 'He': Gender and the Historiography of the European Witch-Hunts." *Journal of Women's History* 7 (fall 1995): 77–101.

Zika, Charles. *Witches and Witch-Hunting in European Societies: A Working Bibliography.* Melbourne: History Department, University of Melbourne, 1998.

CONJURING A NIGHTMARE

The Basque Witch Hunt

Charpentier, Josane. *La sorcellerie en pays Basque.* Paris: Librairie Guénégaud, 1977.

de Lancre, Pierre. *Tableau de l'inconstance des mauvais anges et démons,* 1612. http://www.witchcraft.psmedia.com.

Henningsen, Gustav. *The Witches' Advocate: Basque Witchcraft and the Spanish Inquisition (1609–1614).* Reno: University of Nevada Press, 1980.

Pearl, Jonathan L. *The Crime of Crimes: Demonology and Politics in France 1560–1620.* Waterloo, Ont.: Wilfrid Laurier University Press, 1999.

Robbins, Rossell Hope. *The Encyclopedia of Witchcraft and Demonology.* New York: Crown Publishers, 1974.

Williams, Gerhild Scholz. *Defining Dominion: The Discourses of Magic and Witchcraft in Early Modern France and Germany.* Ann Arbor: University of Michigan Press, 1995.

Theorizing the Witch

Behringer, Wolfgang. "Witchcraft Studies in Austria, Germany and Switzerland." In *Witchcraft in Early Modern Europe: Studies in Culture and Belief,* edited by Jonathan Barry et al., pp. 64–95. Cambridge: Cambridge University Press, 1996.

Boguet, Henry. *An Examen of Witches.* Edited by Montague Summers. 1929. Reprint, London: Frederick Muller, 1971.

Brauer, Sigrid. *Fearless Wives and Frightened Shrews: The Construction of the Witch in Early Modern Germany.* Amherst: University of Massachusetts Press, 1995.

Clark, Stuart. *Thinking With Demons: The Idea of Witchcraft in Early Modern Europe.* Oxford: Clarendon Press, 1997.

Dolan, Frances. "'Ridiculous Fictions': Making Distinctions in the Discourses of Witchcraft." *Differences: A Journal of Feminist Cultural Studies* 7 (1995): 82–110.

Ginzburg, Carlo. *Ecstasies: Deciphering the Witches' Sabbath.* Translated by Raymond Rosenthal. New York: Penguin, 1992.

———. *The Night Battles: Witchcraft and Agrarian Cults in the Sixteenth*

and Seventeeth Centuries. Translated by John Tedeschi and Anne
  Tedeschi. London: Routledge and Kegan Paul, 1983.

Goode, Erich, and Nachman Ben-Yehuda. Moral Panics: The
  Social Construction of Deviance. Oxford: Blackwell, 1994.

Harner, Michael J. "The Role of Hallucinogenic Plants in
  European Witchcraft." In Hallucinogens and Shamanism, edited
  by Michael J. Harner, pp. 125–50. New York: Oxford
  University Press, 1973.

Hester, Marianne. Lewd Women and Wicked Witches: A Study of the
  Dynamics of Male Domination. London: Routledge, 1992.

Kors, Alan C., and Edward Peters, eds. Witchcraft in Europe,
  1100–1700: A Documentary History. Philadelphia: University of
  Pennsylvania Press, 1972.

Kramer, Heinrich, and James Sprenger. Malleus Maleficarum.
  Translated and edited by Montague Summers. 1928.
  Reprint, New York: Dover, 1971.

Larner, Christina. Enemies of God: The Witch-Hunt in Scotland.
  Baltimore: Johns Hopkins University Press, 1981.

———. Witchcraft and Religion: The Politics of Popular Belief. London:
  Basil Blackwell, 1984.

Lea, Henry Charles. Materials Toward a History of Witchcraft.
  Philadelphia: University of Pennsylvania Press, 1939.

Russell, Jeffrey B. A History of Witchcraft: Sorcerers, Heretics, and
  Pagans. London: Thames and Hudson, 1981.

Wiltenburg, Joy. Disorderly Women and Female Power in the Street
  Literature of Early Modern England and Germany. Charlottesville:
  University Press of Virginia, 1992.

The Diabolical Witch in Art

Davidson, Jane P. The Witch in Northern European Art 1470–1750.
  Freren: Luca, 1987.

Dresen-Coenders, Lène. "Witches as Devils' Concubines." In
Saints and She-Devils: Images of Women in the 15th and 16th
  Centuries, edited by Lène Dresen-Coenders, pp. 59–82.
  London: Rubicon, 1987.

Hults, Linda C. "Baldung and the Witches of Freiburg: The
  Evidence of Images." Journal of Interdisciplinary History 18
  (1987): 249–76.

Neave, Dorinda. "The Witch in Early 16th-Century German
  Art." Woman's Art Journal 9 (1988): 3–9.

Préaud, Maxime. Les sorcières. Paris: Bibliothèque Nationale, 1973.

Salerno, Luigi. "Four Witchcraft Scenes by Salvatore Rosa."
  Cleveland Museum of Art Bulletin 65 (1978): 224–31.

Zika, Charles. "Fears of Flying: Representations of Witchcraft
  and Sexuality in Early Sixteenth-Century Germany."
  Australian Journal of Art 8 (1989): 19–47.

The Medieval Backdrop

Chaucer, Geoffrey. "The Wife of Bath's Tale." In The Works of
  Geoffrey Chaucer, edited by F. N. Robinson, pp. 76–88. Boston:
  Houghton Mifflin, 1957.

Cohn, Norman. Europe's Inner Demons: The Demonization of Christians
  in Medieval Christendom. 1973. Reprint, London: Pimlico, 1993.

Flint, Valerie I. J. The Rise of Magic in Early Medieval Europe.
  Princeton: Princeton University Press, 1991.

Gurevich, Aron. Medieval Popular Culture: Problems of Belief and
  Perception. Translated by Janos M. Bak and Paul A.
  Hollingsworth. Cambridge: Cambridge University Press,
  1988.

Henningsen, Gustav. "'The Ladies from Outside': An Archaic
  Pattern of the Witches' Sabbath." In Early Modern European Witch-
  craft: Centres and Peripheries, edited by Bengt Ankarloo and Gustav
  Henningsen, pp. 191–215. Oxford: Clarendon Press, 1990.

Kors, Alan C., and Edward Peters, eds. Witchcraft in Europe,

1100–1700: A Documentary History. Philadelphia: University of Pennsylvania Press, 1972.

Levack, Brian P., ed. *Witchcraft in the Ancient World and the Middle Ages.* New York: Garland, 1992.

Russell, Jeffrey Burton. *Witchcraft in the Middle Ages.* Ithaca: Cornell University Press, 1972.

Seligmann, Kurt. *The History of Magic.* New York: Quality Paperback Book Club, 1997.

Witches and Healers

Achterberg, Jeanne. *Woman As Healer.* Boston: Shambala, 1991.

Briggs, K. M. *Pale Hecate's Team: An Examination of the Beliefs on Witchcraft and Magic among Shakespeare's Contemporaries and His Immediate Successors.* London: Routledge and Kegan Paul, 1962.

Davies, Owen. "Healing Charms in Use in England and Wales 1700–1950." *Folklore* 107 (1996): 19–32.

Harley, David. "Historians as Demonologists: The Myth of the Mid-Wife Witch." *Social History of Medicine* 3 (1990): 1–26.

Hughes, Muriel Joy. *Women Healers in Medieval Life and Literature.* 1943. Reprint, Freeport, N.Y.: Books for Libraries Press, 1968.

O'Neil, Mary. "Magical Healing, Love Magic and the Inquisition in Late Sixteenth-Century Modena." In *Inquisition and Society in Early Modern Europe,* edited and translated by Stephen Haliczer, pp. 88–114. London: Croom Helm, 1987.

Scully, Sally. "Marriage or a Career? Witchcraft as an Alternative in Seventeenth-Century Venice." *Journal of Social History* 28 (1995): 857–76.

The Witch Craze and the Reformation

Burke, Peter. *Popular Culture in Early Modern Europe.* New York: Harper Torchbooks, 1978.

Monter, E. William. *Ritual, Myth and Magic in Early Modern Europe.* Athens, Ohio: Ohio University Press, 1984.

———. *Witchcraft in France and Switzerland: The Borderlands During the Reformation.* Ithaca: Cornell University Press, 1976.

Muchembled, Robert. *Popular Culture and Elite Culture in France 1400–1750.* Translated by Lydia Cochrane. Baton Rouge: Louisiana State University Press, 1978.

———. "The Witches of the Cambrésis: The Acculturation of the Rural World in the Sixteenth and Seventeenth Centuries." *Religion and the People, 800–1700,* edited by James Obelkevich, pp. 221–76. Chapel Hill: University of North Carolina Press, 1979.

Ogier, Darryl. "Night Revels and Werewolfery in Calvinist Guernsey." *Folklore* 109 (1998): 53–62.

Roper, Lyndal. *Oedipus and the Devil: Witchcraft, Sexuality and Religion in Early Modern Europe.* London: Routledge, 1994.

Scribner, Robert W. "The Reformation, Popular Magic, and the 'Disenchantment of the World.'" *Journal of Interdisciplinary History* 23 (1993): 475–94.

Sharpe, James. *Instruments of Darkness: Witchcraft in England 1550–1750.* London: Hamish Hamilton, 1996.

Williams, Selma R. *Riding the Nightmare: Women and Witchcraft from the Old World to Colonial Salem.* New York: Harper, 1992.

OLD WIVES' TALES

The Case of the Lancashire Witches

Barber, Laird H. *An Edition of "The Late Lancashire Witches" by Thomas Heywood and Richard Brome.* New York: Garland, 1979.

Hutchinson, Francis. *An Historical Essay Concerning Witchcraft.* London, 1720. http://www.witchcraft.psmedia.com.

Peel, Edgar, and Pat Southern. *The Trials of the Lancashire Witches.* Newton Abbot: David and Charles, 1969.

Sharpe, James. *Instruments of Darkness: Witchcraft in England 1550–1750*. London: Hamish Hamilton, 1996.

Webster, John. *The Displaying of Supposed Witchcraft*. London, 1677. http://www.witchcraft.psmedia.com.

Neighbor Against Neighbor

Briggs, Robin. *Witches and Neighbors: The Social and Cultural Context of European Witchcraft*. New York: Viking, 1996.

Darnton, Robert. *The Great Cat Massacre and Other Episodes in French Cultural History*. New York: Basic Books, 1984.

Dolan, Frances E. *Dangerous Familiars: Representations of Domestic Crime in England, 1550–1700*. Ithaca: Cornell University Press, 1994.

Goodare, Julian. "Women and the Witch-Hunt in Scotland." *Social History* 23 (1998): 288–308.

Gregory, Annabel. "Witchcraft, Politics and 'Good Neighbourhood' in Early Seventeenth-Century Rye." *Past and Present* 133 (1991): 31–66.

Hindle, Steve. "The Shaming of Margaret Knowsley: Gossip, Gender and the Experience of Authority in Early Modern England." *Continuity and Change* 9 (1994): 391–419.

Holmes, Clive. "Women: Witnesses and Witches." *Past and Present* 140 (1993): 45–78.

Ingram, Martin. "'Scolding Women Cucked or Washed': A Crisis in Gender Relations in Early Modern England?" In *Women, Crime and the Courts in Early Modern England*, edited by Jenny Kermode and Garthine Walker, pp. 48–80. London: UCL Press, 1994.

Purkiss, Diane. *The Witch in History: Early Modern and Twentieth-Century Representations*. London: Routledge, 1996.

Thomas, Keith. *Religion and the Decline of Magic*. New York: Charles Scribner's Sons, 1972.

Underdown, D. E. "The Taming of the Scold: The Enforce-ment of Patriarchal Authority in Early Modern England." In *Order and Disorder in Early Modern England*, edited by Anthony Fletcher and John Stevenson, pp. 116–36. Cambridge: Cambridge University Press, 1985.

Willis, Deborah. *Malevolent Nurture: Witch-Hunting and Maternal Power in Early Modern England*. Ithaca: Cornell University Press, 1995.

Witches and Renaissance Folklore

Briggs, K. M. *Pale Hecate's Team: An Examination of the Beliefs on Witchcraft and Magic among Shakespeare's Contemporaries and His Immediate Successors*. London: Routledge and Kegan Paul, 1962.

Guiley, Rosemary Ellen. *The Encyclopedia of Witches and Witchcraft*. New York: Facts on File, 1989.

Henningsen, Gustav. "Witchcraft." In *Folklore: An Encyclopedia of Beliefs, Customs, Tales, Music, and Art*, edited by Thomas A. Green, pp. 842–48. Santa Barbara: ABC-Clio, 1997.

Morris, Katherine. *Sorceress or Witch? The Image of Gender in Medieval Iceland and Northern Europe*. New York: University Press of America, 1991.

Newall, Venetia, ed. *The Witch Figure: Folklore Essays by a Group of Scholars in England Honouring the 75th Birthday of Katharine M. Briggs*. London: Routledge and Kegan Paul, 1973.

Nildin-Wall, Bodil, and Jan Wall. "The Witch as Hare or the Witch's Hare: Popular Legends and Beliefs in Nordic Tradition." *Folklore* 104 (1993): 67–85.

Simpson, Jacqueline. *European Mythology*. London: Peter Bedrick Books, 1987.

———. "Witches and Witchbusters." *Folklore* 107 (1996): 5–18.

Science and Skepticism

Baroja, Julio Caro. "Witchcraft and Catholic Theology." In

Early Modern European Witchcraft: Centres and Peripheries, edited by Bengt Ankarloo and Gustav Henningsen, pp. 19–44. Oxford: Clarendon Press, 1990.

Bostridge, Ian. *Witchcraft and Its Transformations c. 1650–1750.* Oxford: Clarendon Press, 1997.

Clark, Stuart. *Thinking With Demons: The Idea of Witchcraft in Early Modern Europe.* Oxford: Clarendon Press, 1997.

Leventhal, Herbert. *In the Shadow of the Enlightenment: Occultism and Renaissance Science in Eighteenth-Century America.* New York: New York University Press, 1976.

Monter, E. William. *Witchcraft in France and Switzerland: The Borderlands During the Reformation.* Ithaca: Cornell University Press, 1976.

Notestein, Wallace. *A History of Witchcraft in England from 1558 to 1718.* 1911. Reprint, New York: Russell and Russell, 1965.

Scot, Reginald. *The Discoverie of Witchcraft.* London, 1584. http://www.witchcraft.psmedia.com.

Sharpe, James. *Instruments of Darkness: Witchcraft in England 1550–1750.* London: Hamish Hamilton, 1996.

Weyer, Johann. *Witches, Devils and Doctors in the Renaissance [De praestigiis daemonum].* Binghamton, N.Y.: Medieval and Renaissance Texts and Studies, 1991.

Possession and Hysteria

Allison, David B., and Mark S. Roberts. "On Constructing the Disorder of Hysteria." *Journal of Medicine and Philosophy* 19 (1994): 239–59.

Dijkstra, Bram. *Evil Sisters: The Threat of Female Sexuality in Twentieth-Century Culture.* New York: Henry Holt, 1996.

———. *Idols of Perversity: Fantasies of Feminine Evil in Fin-de-Siècle Culture.* New York: Oxford University Press, 1986.

Evans, Martha Noel. *Fits and Starts: A Genealogy of Hysteria in*

Modern France. Ithaca: Cornell University Press, 1991.

Geis, Gilbert, and Ivan Bunn. *A Trial of Witches: A Seventeenth-Century Witchcraft Prosecution.* London: Routledge, 1997.

MacDonald, Michael, ed. *Witchcraft and Hysteria in Elizabethan London: Edward Jorden and the Mary Glover Case.* London: Tavistock/Routledge, 1991.

Séguin, Robert-Lionel. *La sorcellerie au Canada français du XVIIe au XIXe siècles.* Montréal: Librarie Ducharme, 1958.

Veith, Ilza. *Hysteria: The History of a Disease.* Chicago: University of Chicago Press, 1966.

Walker, D. P. *Unclean Spirits: Possession and Exorcism in France and England in the Late Sixteenth and Early Seventeenth Centuries.* Philadelphia: University of Pennsylvania Press, 1981.

Salem

Demos, John Putnam. *Entertaining Satan: Witchcraft and the Culture of Early New England.* Oxford: Oxford University Press, 1982.

Gragg, Larry. "Under an Evil Hand." *American History Illustrated* (March/April 1992), pp. 54–59.

Karlsen, Carol F. *The Devil in the Shape of a Woman: Witchcraft in Colonial New England.* New York: W. W. Norton, 1987.

Klaits, Joseph. *Servants of Satan: The Age of the Witch Hunts.* Bloomington: Indiana University Press, 1985.

ROMANCING THE WITCH

Fairy tales and Their Tellers

Leinweber, David Walter. "Witchcraft and Lamiae in 'The Golden Ass.'" *Folklore* 105 (1994): 77–82.

Mitford, Nancy. *The Sun King.* London: Hamish Hamilton, 1966.

Opie, Iona and Peter Opie. *The Classic Fairy Tales.* London: Oxford University Press, 1974.

Seifert, Lewis C. *Fairy Tales, Sexuality, and Gender in France 1690–1715: Nostalgic Utopias.* Cambridge: Cambridge University Press, 1996.

Warner, Marina. *From the Beast to the Blonde: On Fairy Tales and Their Tellers.* London: Vintage, 1995.

——, ed. *Wonder Tales: Six Stories of Enchantment.* London: Vintage, 1996.

Zipes, Jack, ed. *Beauties, Beasts and Enchantment: Classic French Fairy Tales.* New York: New American Library, 1989.

——. *Fairy Tales and the Art of Subversion: The Classic Genre for Children and the Process of Civilization.* New York: Wildman Press, 1983.

——. *Spells of Enchantment: The Wondrous Fairy Tales of Western Culture.* New York: Viking, 1991.

The Brothers Grimm

Bottigheimer, Ruth B. "From Gold to Guilt: The Forces Which Reshaped *Grimms' Tales.*" In *The Brothers Grimm and Folktale,* edited by James M. McGlathery, pp. 192–204. Chicago: University of Illinois Press, 1988.

——. *Grimms' Bad Girls and Bold Boys: The Moral and Social Vision of the Tales.* New Haven: Yale University Press, 1987.

——. "Transformed Queen: A Search for the Origins of Negative Female Archetypes in Grimms' Fairy Tales." *Amsterdamer Beiträge zur neueren Germanistik* 10 (1980): 1–12.

The Complete Grimms' Fairy Tales. London: Routledge and Kegan Paul, 1975.

Ellis, John M. *One Fairy Story Too Many: The Brothers Grimm and Their Tales.* Chicago: University of Chicago Press, 1983.

Lundell, Torborg. *Fairy Tale Mothers.* New York: Peter Lang, 1990.

Simpson, Jacqueline. *European Mythology.* London: Peter Bedrick Books, 1987.

Tatar, Maria. *The Hard Facts of the Grimms' Fairy Tales.* Princeton: Princeton University Press, 1987.

——. *Off With Their Heads! Fairytales and the Culture of Childhood.* Princeton: Princeton University Press, 1992.

Zipes, Jack. *The Brothers Grimm: From Enchanted Forests to the Modern World.* New York: Routledge, 1988.

Witches and Romanticism

Leland, Charles G. *Aradia: The Gospel of the Witches.* 1899. Reprint, London: C. W. Daniel, 1974.

Marsh, Jan. *Pre-Raphaelite Women: Images of Femininity.* New York: Harmony Books, 1987.

Marsh, Jan, and Pamela Gerrish Nunn. *Women Artists and the Pre-Raphaelite Movement.* London: Virago, 1989.

Michelet, Jules. *La sorcière.* 1862. Reprint, Paris: Librarie Marcel Didier, 1952.

Morgan, Thaïs E., ed. *Victorian Sages and Cultural Discourse: Renegotiating Gender and Power.* London: Rutgers University Press, 1990.

Parris, Leslie, ed. *The Pre-Raphaelites.* London: Tate Gallery Publications, 1994.

Williams, Anne. *Art of Darkness: A Poetics of Gothic.* Chicago: University of Chicago Press, 1995.

Wilson, Colin. *The Occult: A History.* New York: Vintage Books, 1973.

Margaret Murray

M. A. M. [Margaret Alice Murray]. "Witchcraft." *Encyclopaedia Britannica* 23 (1929, 14th ed.): 686–88.

Mallowan, Max. "Murray, M. A." *Dictionary of National Biography 1961–1970,* edited by E. T. Williams and C. S. Nicholls, pp. 777–78. Oxford: Oxford University Press, 1981.

Murray, Margaret A. *The God of the Witches.* Oxford: Oxford
University Press, 1933.

———. *My First Hundred Years.* London: William Kimber, 1963.

———. *The Witch-Cult in Western Europe: A Study in Anthropology.*
1921. Reprint, Oxford: Oxford University Press, 1962.

Simpson, Jacqueline. "Margaret Murray: Who Believed Her,
and Why?" *Folklore* 105 (1994): 89–96.

Witches and (Neo)Pagans

Dupont-Buchat, Marie-Sylvie. "Le diable apprivoisé, la sorcellerie revisitée: magie et sorcellerie au XIXe siècle." In *Magie et
sorcellerie en Europe du moyen age à nos jours,* edited by Robert
Muchembled, pp. 235–66. Paris: Armand Colin, 1994.

Hutton, Ronald. *The Pagan Religions of the Ancient British Isles: Their
Nature and Legacy.* Oxford: Blackwell, 1991.

———. *The Stations of the Sun: A History of the Ritual Year in Britain.*
Oxford: Oxford University Press, 1997.

Jones, Prudence, and Nigel Pennick. *A History of Pagan Europe.*
London: Routledge, 1995.

LIFTING THE CURSE

Feminism and Wicca

Bovenschen, Silvia. "The Contemporary Witch, the Historical
Witch and the Witch Myth: The Witch, Subject of the
Appropriation of Nature and Object of the Domination of
Nature." *New German Critique* 15 (fall 1978): 83–119.

Gage, Matilda Joslyn. *Woman, Church and State.* 1893. Reprint,
New York: Arno Press, 1972.

Hasted, Rachel. "Mothers of Invention." *Trouble and Strife* 7
(winter 1985): 17–25.

Morgan, Robin, ed. *Sisterhood Is Powerful: An Anthology of Writings*
from the Women's Liberation Movement. New York: Vintage, 1970.

Orion, Loretta. *Never Again the Burning Times: Paganism Revived.*
Prospect Heights, Ill.: Waveland Press, 1995.

Reis, Elizabeth, ed. *Spellbound: Women and Witchcraft in America.*
Wilmington, Del.: Scholarly Resources, 1998.

Starhawk. *Dreaming the Dark: Magic, Sex and Politics.* 1982.
Reprint, Boston: Beacon, 1988.

———. *The Spiral Dance: A Rebirth of the Ancient Religion of the Great
Goddess.* 1979. Reprint, San Francisco: Harper and Row,
1989.

———. *Truth or Dare: Encounters with Power, Authority and Mystery.*
San Francisco: Harper Collins, 1987.

Wolstein, Diane, and Samuel Noah Kramer. *Inanna, Queen of
Heaven and Earth: Her Stories and Hymns from Sumer.* London:
Rider, 1983.

INDEX